Discovering

Londo

Fami

GW00696032

Peter Matthews

The Lord Mayor's coach with his guard of pikemen in the Lord Mayor's Show.

A Shire book

British Library Cataloguing in Publication Data: Matthews, Peter. Discovering London for families 1. Family recreation – England – London – Guidebooks 2. London (England) – Guidebooks I. Title 914.2'1'0486. ISBN 0 7478 0505 9.

Front cover: *The London Eye, with the Houses of Parliament in the background.*

Back cover: *Changing the guard at Horse Guards.*

The information in this book was believed to be correct at the time of publication. However, changes may occur (especially in opening times) and readers wishing to see particular items are advised to confirm the details, using the telephone numbers or websites listed, before they travel.

ACKNOWLEDGEMENTS
The author and publishers are grateful to those organisations which have supplied photographs and permitted their publication here. Photographs are acknowledged as follows: copyright Nicholas Kane, page 39; copyright Andrew Putler, page 28; the Imperial War Museum, page 83 (bottom); the London Aquarium, page 86 (both); Madame Tussaud's, page 67 (both); Madame Tussaud's Rock Circus, page 38; copyright Museum of London, page 60; the National Gallery, pages 30 and 32; the Natural History Museum, page 71; the Science Museum, page 74; the V&A Picture Library, pages 75 and 101.
    Cartography by Robert Dizon.

Published in 2001 by Shire Publications Ltd, Cromwell House, Church Street, Princes Risborough, Buckinghamshire HP27 9AA, UK. (Website: www.shirebooks.co.uk) Copyright © 2001 by Peter Matthews. First published 2001. Number 293 in the Discovering series. ISBN 0 7478 0505 9.

Printed in Malta by Gutenberg Press Limited, Gudja Road, Tarxien PLA19, Malta.

Contents

A pavement artist at work on the South Bank.

Introduction

There is so much to see and do in London that some preparation is essential. From the air or a train it seems to be a vast urban sprawl, but fortunately most of the capital's attractions are to be found at its heart, in the City, Westminster, Southwark or Kensington. London can, however, be a confusing place, so do buy a good map before or soon after you arrive. The A–Z is probably the best-known, with a range of maps to suit all needs, but there are many other maps on the market, of which those published by Benson Maps or HarperCollins, both fairly widely available, are among the clearest.

This book is arranged, for the most part, geographically so that you can combine, for example, a walk down Whitehall with a visit to the National Gallery or National Portrait Gallery. Full details for each attraction are given after the description, including opening hours, telephone numbers, travel information and websites, where available. Many attractions now have their own website, giving lots of information on what you can see and what special events and exhibitions are on, and it is worth exploring them before you leave home. Admission charges are not listed, as they usually change on an annual basis, but we do tell you when there is a charge. We also tell you which attractions offer free admission for children and senior citizens, or free admission one day a week or after 16.30. Many museums, galleries and attractions offer discounts for groups, usually of more than ten people. It is best to telephone in advance to check as many of them limit the number of groups allowed in each day. Pre-booked school groups are usually allowed in free, and most places have useful information packs available to help you get the most out of a visit. Following a change in the tax laws, it is highly likely that several of the major charging museums will be free to all visitors by the end of 2001.

As you walk around London you will notice circular blue plaques attached to many buildings. They commemorate famous people from all walks of life who once lived there, including writers, artists, musicians, scientists and statesmen. For more information see Further Reading at the end of the book.

GETTING AROUND

Unless you have to, driving around London is not recommended. The streets are very congested and parking is both difficult and expensive. If you park illegally you may have your car clamped or removed, which means wasting valuable time as well as paying a fee for it to be released. If you are bringing your car to London for a day trip it would be best to leave it at an outlying Underground or rail station, many of which have car parks, and continue your journey by public transport.

The London Underground, more commonly called the Tube, is the world's oldest underground railway system. It is also one of the most extensive, with twelve lines serving the majority of the capital, especially north of the Thames. It does not always offer the most efficient service owing to the demands put on it, but for a first-time visitor it is the simplest way to get around. To help you plan your journey, ask for a Tube map at any station. There are six zones, Zone 1 being the central area within the Circle Line. Various Travelcards are available for travel within the zones, valid for one day, a week or a month. For the weekly and monthly tickets you will need a photograph for a photocard. The further you travel across the zones, the more expensive the ticket. Travelcards can also be used on buses. Travelcards are well worth investing in, for the convenience as well as the saving, but bear in mind that the one-day card is not valid on Mondays to Fridays until after 9.30. There is also a one-day Family Travelcard which is valid for groups of one or two adults plus between one and four children. This offers even more savings but the group must travel together. Tickets can be bought at any Tube station or the Travel Information

Centres listed below. There are also Visitor Travelcards for three, four or seven days available only through travel agents and tour operators outside London, usually as part of a package.

You must have a ticket *before* you travel on the Tube. Many stations, especially in the centre, now have automated barriers. You put your ticket face up into the slot and take it out of the top of the machine for the barrier to open. If it fails to work ask a member of staff to help you. Each of the Tube lines is colour-coded. When you want to change lines look for the coloured signs pointing you in the right direction. The Tube runs from about 5.30 (7.00 on Sundays) until around midnight. The two busiest periods (the 'rush hours') are from 7.30 to 9.30 in the morning and from 17.00 to 19.00 in the evening, when London's workers are on their way to and from work. It is best to avoid these times if possible, especially if you have luggage or a pushchair.

You can also use your Travelcard on the Docklands Light Railway, which takes you in and around the redeveloped area of the old docks. The system connects with the main Underground network at Bank, and Tower Gateway station is very close to Tower Hill Underground station. The trains all run above ground; it is an interesting experience to glide in between the mix of old and new buildings that make up this historic part of the East End. All the trains are computer-operated and there is no driver, though a member of staff is always on hand. The service has been extended beneath the river Thames to Greenwich and on to Lewisham in south-east London.

Perhaps the best way to get to know London is to travel by bus, especially in the front seat on the top deck, from where you get the best views. Many of London's buses are now of the modern enclosed variety with a driver and no conductor, but a number of routes which run through the centre still use the famous Routemasters, with an open rear platform and a conductor to issue tickets and call out the various stops. Although the routes are now operated by private companies, Transport for London (which has replaced London Transport) is still in overall control of the buses and they all accept Travelcards. (Deregulation also explains why many of the buses are no longer red.) The fare structure on the buses is simpler than that on the Tube. There are two zones and two prices: an outer zone with a cheaper fare and a central zone where the fare is slightly dearer. The central zone covers much the same area as Zone 1 on the Tube. There are two kinds of bus stop. A white stop denotes a fare stage, at which all buses stop, unless they are full. A red stop means it is a request stop, where you must put out your hand for the bus to stop; if you are on the bus you need to ring the bell in good time for the driver to know to stop for you.

For information on London's Tube and bus services there is a 24-hour telephone service on 020 7222 1234 and a useful website, www.londontransport.co.uk. There are also Travel Information Centres at the Underground stations at St James's Park, King's Cross, Liverpool Street, Oxford Circus and Piccadilly Circus, as well as at Euston, Victoria and Paddington railway stations.

A good way to get your bearings if you have not been to London before is to take one of the open-top bus tours which do a circuit of the main sights. You can either stay on the bus for the whole tour or use your ticket to hop on and off throughout the day. Two companies run these tours: The Original London Sightseeing Tour (020 8877 1722, www.theoriginaltour.com); and The Big Bus Company (020 7233 9533, www.bigbus.co.uk). Their brochures are available from Tourist Information Centres (see page 8). More detailed guided tours with qualified Blue Badge guides are also available. These sometimes include a guided visit to some of the main attractions or a river trip. Companies offering these tours are Evan Evans (020 7950 1777, www.evanevans.co.uk); Golden Tours (020 7233 7030, www.goldentours.co.uk), and Frames Rickards (020 7837 3111, www.bitoa.co.uk/frames.htm). Brochures are available from Tourist Information Centres, or contact the companies direct. For a rather more unusual tour you could try Frog Tours, who drive you around in converted Second World War DUKW amphibious vehicles which can drive into the

Thames for a river cruise as well. Tours start from Belvedere Road, near the London Eye; it is advisable to book, especially for weekends (020 7928 3132, www.frogtours.com).

Although rather more expensive, a trip in a taxi can sometimes be the most convenient way to travel. Although London's 'black cabs' are now painted in all sorts of different colours and are often covered in advertising, their distinctive shape is easily recognisable. A London taxi driver really knows his way around the capital as he will have done 'the knowledge' – spent at least two years riding around on a moped getting to know all the main routes and backroads before being given his coveted badge.

Another excellent way to see London is from the river Thames, especially as so many new attractions have sprung up along its banks. Pleasure boats operate from Westminster, Embankment and Tower piers and the boats leave fairly regularly. The most popular ride is the short round trip from Westminster to the City and you can also go downstream to Greenwich, passing all the new developments in Docklands. It is even possible to go as far as Hampton Court but the journey can be as long as four hours, depending on the tide, and boats do not go upstream after the end of October.

Last but not least, you can see London on foot, and guided walking tours are now proving highly popular. Walks include tours of the East End, the London of Charles Dickens, museum and gallery tours and, if you are feeling brave, ghost walks and the rather more gory Jack the Ripper tour. There is no need to book – you simply turn up at the meeting point. All walks take place regardless of the weather. Leaflets can be picked up at Tourist Information Centres. Two of the more established companies are London Walks (020 7624 9255, www.walks.com) and Historical Walks of London (020 8668 4019). With both companies, children under fourteen go free if accompanied by an adult.

SHOPPING AND PLACES TO EAT

London is a great place to shop, with lots of opportunities to look for bargains or the latest fashions. London's best-known shopping street is Oxford Street, which stretches for a mile (1.6 km) from Marble Arch to Tottenham Court Road. Here you will find famous stores such as John Lewis, Marks & Spencer and Selfridges, the massive music shops HMV and Virgin, and smaller independent shops of all sorts. Do beware of the unlicensed pavement salesmen who claim to be selling brand-name perfumes, watches and the like at ridiculously cheap prices: the products may well be fake. Regent Street is another good shopping street, with two great stores popular with children (see Chapter 9). More up-market stores such as Harvey Nichols and Harrods are to be found in Knightsbridge. London also has many excellent street markets offering a wide range of goods (see Chapter 27).

There are plenty of places to eat in London, with most of the world's cuisines on offer somewhere or other. For those in a hurry there are many fast-food outlets such as sandwich bars or burger bars. In the West End, especially in Soho, you will find reasonably priced Italian, Indian or Chinese restaurants as well as the more expensive 'themed' restaurants, such as Planet Hollywood and the Hard Rock Cafe. Many of London's attractions now have their own cafe or restaurant.

There are several good restaurant and shopping guides on the market, including Harden's *Good Cheap Eats in London* and *Time Out*'s annually updated *London Shopping Guide*. These can be found in most good bookshops. You may also like to visit the shop at the Museum of London, which has these and many more books on London for both children and adults.

Finally, a word of warning. Like any major city, London can get very crowded, especially in or around popular attractions, at major events, street markets and on the Underground. Unfortunately, crowds attract pickpockets and thieves, so do keep your valuables hidden and bags closed at all times. A little care will ensure a happy visit.

A summer's day in St James's Park.

TOURIST INFORMATION

For further help and advice during a trip to London you may like to visit one of the following Tourist Information Centres.

Victoria station forecourt, SW1. Open Monday to Saturday 8.00–19.00, Sunday 8.00–18.15. Extended hours from Easter to October.

Liverpool Street station, EC2. Open Monday to Friday 8.00–18.00, Saturday 8.00–17.30, Sunday 9.00–17.30.

Heathrow Terminals 1, 2, 3 Underground station. Open 8.00–18.00.

Southwark Information Centre, London Bridge, SE1. Telephone: 020 7403 8299. Open: November to Easter, Monday to Saturday 10.00–16.00, Sunday 11.00–16.00; Easter to October, Monday to Saturday 10.00–18.00, Sunday 10.30–17.30.

City of London Information Centre, St Paul's Churchyard, EC4. Telephone: 020 7332 1456. Open Monday to Friday 9.30–17.00, Saturday 9.30–12.30.

Greenwich Tourist Information Centre, Pepys House, 2 Cutty Sark Gardens, SE10. Telephone: 0870 608 2000. Open: September to June, 10.00–17.00; July to August, 10.00–20.00.

Britain Visitor Centre, 1 Regent Street, SW1. Open: Monday 9.30–18.30, Tuesday to Friday 9.00–18.30, Saturday and Sunday 10.00–16.00 (Saturday, June to October 9.00–17.00).

The London Tourist Board's website (www.LondonTown.com) has lots of good information on attractions, events, accommodation and entertainment. There is also a recorded information service called London Line, which is available twenty-four hours a day, but only within the United Kingdom. The main number is 09068 663344, which allows you to access all sorts of information, from Changing the Guard to Children's London. All calls are charged at the premium rate. You may also find it useful to buy a copy of the weekly magazine *Time Out* for its detailed listings of what is on at cinemas and theatres, as well as special children's events.

1
Major events in London

Whatever time of year you visit London you will find there are special events of all kinds going on, from pageantry to sports, and many of them are free. The following will help you time your visit to coincide with a particular event or make sure you do not miss something when you do come. Contact telephone numbers are given where applicable for further information or to book tickets. Information is also available from Tourist Information Centres (see opposite page), the London Tourist Board's London Line telephone service of pre-recorded information (09068 663344), or on its website (www.LondonTown.com).

DAILY EVENTS

Changing the Guard takes place at Buckingham Palace at 11.30, daily from April to July but on alternate days the rest of the year. The whole ceremony lasts about 35 minutes. It is very popular, especially in summer, so you need to arrive early to get a good view. In wet weather it may be cancelled, and times vary when important state events take place. Telephone 09068 353718 to check. (For a more detailed description of the ceremony see Chapter 8.)

Changing the Guard at Horse Guards takes place at 11.00 from Monday to Saturday and at 10.00 on Sunday. The ceremony lasts about 25 minutes. Times may change during state events, so check on the number given above.

Every night for the last seven hundred years the **Ceremony of the Keys** has taken place at the Tower of London. This short but moving ceremony is carried out by the Chief Yeoman Warder, who, accompanied by an escort of Guards, locks the main gates to the Tower a little before 22.00. It is possible to attend the ceremony if you request passes well in advance. Write, enclosing a stamped addressed envelope, to: Operations Department, HM Tower of London, London EC3N 4AB.

Several times a year **gun salutes** are carried out in Hyde Park and at the Tower of London on state occasions such as royal birthdays, Trooping the Colour and to welcome important visitors. The sound of the guns booms out across London. Salutes in Hyde Park take place at 12.00 opposite the Dorchester Hotel and are performed by the King's Troop Royal Horse Artillery. Salutes at the Tower are fired at 13.00 on Tower Wharf by the Honourable Artillery Company. Dates when you can expect a gun salute are 6th February

Changing the Guard at Horse Guards Parade.

9

Chinese New Year celebrations in Leicester Square.

(to celebrate the Queen's accession to the throne), 21st April (the Queen's birthday), 2nd June (Coronation Day) and 10th June (Prince Philip's birthday). More detail is available in the Historic Royal Palaces website, www.hrp.org.uk/index2.htm

ANNUAL EVENTS

January

The New Year's Parade on 1st January claims to be the world's biggest street spectacular, with marching bands, cheerleaders, giant inflatable characters and clowns processing through the streets of central London. The route is from Parliament Square through Trafalgar Square, Piccadilly Circus and on to Berkeley Square. For further information telephone 0900 525 2001 or visit the website on www.londonparade.co.uk.

January-February

Chinese New Year can take place in either January or February as the Chinese calendar has thirteen lunar months. It is usually celebrated on the Sunday following the actual date. The festivities take place in Chinatown in Soho and are centred around Gerrard Street, starting from around 11.00. The whole area is decorated with streamers and flags and traditional music is played. The highlight is the Lion Dance, when young men in a lion costume dance down the street receiving gifts of money from the restaurants and businesses.

March

The **Head of the River Race** is a boat race from Mortlake to Putney. (This is the University Boat Race course in reverse, but there are about four hundred crews instead of just two.) The race lasts about 1 1/2 hours and the best views are from the river bank near Chiswick Bridge.

The **University Boat Race** is one of the world's best-known boat races, rowed by crews from Britain's two oldest universities, Oxford and Cambridge. The two teams race over a course of 4 3/4 miles (7.6 km) from Putney to Mortlake. The best views are probably from Putney and Chiswick bridges.

April

Over 30,000 people take part in the **London Marathon**, including professional runners, athletes in wheelchairs and many amateurs raising money for charity. Millions of pounds are raised every year for good causes. Especially popular are those running in bizarre costumes. The race begins in Greenwich and the route passes through the streets of London to finish in the Mall. Further information on 09068 334450 or www.london-marathon.co.uk.

June

The **Trooping the Colour** ceremony is London's most spectacular piece of royal pageantry. It is held on Horse Guards Parade on a Saturday in June to celebrate the Queen's official birthday. The ceremony comes from the need for soldiers to recognise their regimental colour (or flag) in the heat of battle. Each year a different regiment troops its colour before the Queen as part of a colourful display of highly disciplined marching, complete with massed bands and mounted troops. Tickets are allocated by ballot and you must write in January or February to Brigade Major (Trooping the Colour), Headquarters Household Division, Horse Guards, Whitehall, London SW1A 2AX (020 7414 2479). Otherwise, you can stand on the Mall to watch the procession from Buckingham Palace and back again.

The **Coin Street Festival** takes place from June to September on the South Bank near Gabriel's Wharf. There is music and dance from many different cultures from all round the world, and it is all free. Further information on 020 7401 2255 or www.coinstreetfestival.org.

July

One of the most famous music festivals in the world is the annual series of **Promenade Concerts** (known as the Proms) which take place at the Royal Albert Hall from July to September. Many of the world's best musicians and orchestras take part and the programmes contain a mixture of popular and less well-known music. There are also special concerts for children. You can buy tickets in advance, but to 'prom' (in other words, to stand in the arena in front of the platform or up in the gallery) you need to queue during the day. For further information contact 020 7765 5575.

The **Doggett's Coat and Badge Race** is rowed every July on the Thames between London Bridge and Chelsea by apprentice watermen dressed in their bright red livery. The race is named after Thomas Doggett and was first rowed in 1715. Doggett is said to have been having trouble getting to his home in Chelsea one stormy night and was eventually rowed there in appalling conditions by a young waterman (the equivalent in those days of a taxi driver). He was so impressed that he founded the race, and today's winner is still presented with a special coat and badge.

August

The **Notting Hill Carnival** is one of the world's biggest free street carnivals, attracting many thousands of visitors on the Sunday and Monday of August Bank Holiday. Started in the 1960s by the local black community, it features steel bands, reggae, calypso and some highly colourful and imaginative costumes. Children's Carnival Day is on the Sunday. Further information on 020 8964 0544 or www.nottinghillcarnival.net.uk

October

The **Pearly Harvest Festival Service** takes place on the first Sunday in October at St Martin-in-the-Fields church in Trafalgar Square. This is a great opportunity to see London's pearly kings and queens, dressed in their traditional outfits covered in

Some of the hundreds of cars leaving Hyde Park at the start of the London to Brighton Veteran Car Run.

mother-of-pearl buttons. The service starts at 15.00.

November

On the first Sunday in November the **London to Brighton Veteran Car Run** starts from Hyde Park. About four hundred enthusiasts set out in an impressive array of cars, all of which were made before 1905. Not all the competitors make it to Brighton. It is necessary to get to Hyde Park early as they leave between 7.30 and 9.00, but you can also watch them along the A23 on their way out of London.

On the second Saturday in November the newly elected Lord Mayor of the City of London rides through the streets in the **Lord Mayor's Show**. He is carried in a splendid golden coach to the Law Courts in the Strand, where he pledges his allegiance to the sovereign, after which the procession returns to his official residence at the Mansion House. The parade is one of London's best free spectacles, with lots of marching bands and decorated floats. Further information on 020 7606 3030 or www.lordmayorsshow.org.

On the Sunday nearest to 11th November **Remembrance Sunday** is celebrated at the Cenotaph in Whitehall, usually in the presence of the Queen. After two minutes silence at 11.00, the Queen and others lay wreaths and there is a march-past of war veterans.

In the middle of November the **Christmas lights** are switched on in Oxford Street, Regent Street and Bond Street by celebrities. The lights are illuminated every night from dusk to midnight until 6th January.

December

Early in December a **Christmas tree** donated by the Norwegian city of Oslo is put up in Trafalgar Square. It serves as a focus for Christmas celebrations, with carols sung under the tree every evening to raise money for charity.

The modern reconstruction of Shakespeare's Globe Theatre at Bankside.

2
A brief history of London

The story of London began nearly two thousand years ago when the Romans invaded Britain in AD 43. They found they could ford the river Thames where Westminster is today and they built a small trading town on two hills north of the river, where the City now stands. This was the beginning of *Londinium*, which quickly grew in importance and was made the capital of the province. In about AD 60 Boudicca, queen of the Iceni tribe from East Anglia, burnt the city to the ground before being beaten in battle and killing herself. A statue of her in her war chariot

stands by Westminster Bridge. The Romans built a wooden bridge more or less where London Bridge is now and later protected the city with high walls, some of which can still be seen today. The best section is just outside Tower Hill Underground station and there is more near the Museum of London.

When the Romans left in AD 410 the city was more or less abandoned until Saxon invaders settled outside the walls, in the area around Covent Garden. The first, wooden, St Paul's Cathedral was built inside the walls in AD 604. In the late ninth century London was resettled by Alfred the

The London Eye on the South Bank.

Staple Inn in Holborn is one of the few buildings that survived the Great Fire of London.

Great. London was invaded by Vikings several times over the next two hundred years and in 1014 King Olaf of Norway tried to help the Saxons regain control by tying ropes from his ships to the wooden bridge to pull it down, an event which gave rise to the nursery rhyme 'London Bridge Is Falling Down'.

The penultimate Saxon king, Edward the Confessor, built a new royal palace about a mile upstream of the city at Westminster, which has been the seat of government ever since. He also rebuilt the abbey church, where he was later buried and where his shrine can still be seen.

The first king to be crowned at Westminster Abbey was William the Conqueror in 1066; since then all coronations have taken place there. To defend the city and ensure the subservience of its inhabitants, William built a massive fortress which still stands at the heart of the Tower of London.

Medieval London consisted of lots of wooden buildings in narrow streets. It remained within the old Roman walls. The old bridge was replaced in 1209 by a stone one, which lasted until the 1830s. It had houses and shops along both sides, a chapel in the middle, and the heads of traitors were stuck on poles on the southern gatehouse as a warning to others.

The Tudor period was one of great splendour, with magnificent new royal palaces in Whitehall, St James's and Hampton Court where important visitors were entertained. During the reign of Elizabeth I (1558–1603), several theatres were built on Bankside in Southwark and it was here that many of Shakespeare's plays were first performed. The reconstructed Globe Theatre gives an idea of what Elizabethan theatres were like.

For centuries outbreaks of the plague had killed many thousands. It was carried by fleas on rats, although no-one knew this at the time. In 1665 the Great Plague killed about 100,000 people, a quarter of London's population. Disaster struck again in 1666, when fire broke out in the royal bakery in Pudding Lane and spread rapidly.

The Great Fire, which lasted four days, destroyed four-fifths of London although only about nine people lost their lives. London was rebuilt using stone and brick, as the old wooden buildings had helped the fire spread. Sir Christopher Wren built a new St Paul's Cathedral and many new churches, of which about twenty still survive. Very few buildings from before the Great Fire remain in London; the half-timbered Staple Inn in Holborn is a rare example. Despite the setbacks, London developed into a major trade centre during the seventeenth century.

In the eighteenth century, as the population grew, London became very cramped and people started to move out into new residential areas such as Covent Garden. Many elegant squares were built for the wealthy, especially in the areas of Mayfair and Bloomsbury. The best preserved square is Bedford Square near the British Museum. Growing wealth was accompanied by increased crime, and mass hangings at Tyburn near Marble Arch were a popular form of entertainment.

In the nineteenth century London grew rapidly, helped by the development of the railways and new technology. The first train steamed into London in 1836, the first bus service started in 1829 and the first Underground railway opened in 1863. In 1894 Tower Bridge opened, London's most famous bridge and a masterpiece of Victorian engineering. Britain was an important world power and many impressive new buildings reflected this, including railway stations such as St Pancras and the new Houses of Parliament. In 1851 the Great Exhibition was held in the Crystal Palace in Hyde Park and was a huge success, with six million people visiting it. Some of the profits went towards building the popular South Kensington museums.

London was very much affected by the Second World War, with many Londoners killed or made homeless by the bombings. During the Blitz of 1940 thousands of homes and buildings, especially in the City and East End, were destroyed and many Londoners took shelter in Underground stations.

Since the nineteenth century London had been famous for its fog, especially the smog or 'pea-souper', when it was impossible to see more than a few paces ahead. After a particularly bad winter in 1952 when thousands died, the Clean Air Act was passed, banning the burning of coal and making foggy London a thing of the past.

The arrival of the third millennium has prompted the building of many new landmarks in London, many of them along the banks of the Thames. Perhaps the most recognisable is the Dome at Greenwich. The British Airways London Eye, or Millennium Wheel, offers visitors a spectacular view of the city, and the Millennium Bridge, despite a wobbly start, will be a new pedestrian river crossing. Other projects have included the conversion of the redundant power station at Bankside into a museum of modern art, the Tate Modern, and turning Somerset House in the Strand into a new cultural centre.

3
Westminster Abbey

Westminster Abbey is probably Britain's best-known and best-loved church and has been the scene of many important national occasions. It has many royal connections: kings and queens have been crowned here since 1066; there have been royal weddings here; there have also been royal funerals and the Abbey contains many royal tombs. Another popular attraction of the Abbey are the tombs and memorials to famous politicians, scientists, musicians and writers.

According to legend, King Sebert of the East Saxons built the first church in the very early years of the seventh century in what was then a marshy area known as Thorney Island. There was certainly an abbey here when Edward the Confessor, the last great Saxon king, built a new palace at Westminster. He rebuilt the abbey church; but in 1065, a few days after it was finished, he died and was the first person to be buried in it. Edward died childless and, in the fight for the throne which followed, his cousin William, Duke of Normandy, invaded England and defeated King Harold at the Battle of Hastings. On Christmas Day 1066 William the Conqueror was crowned William I in Westminster Abbey and coronations have taken place here ever since.

Two hundred years later Henry III rebuilt the abbey church. It was designed specifically to hold coronations and to be the burial place of kings. At the heart of the church was the richly decorated shrine of the now canonised Edward the Confessor. Henry was a great builder, but very extravagant; it is said that he once had to pawn the jewels he had given to the shrine, although he later returned them. He was buried next to Edward the Confessor's tomb. Several other medieval kings and queens were buried around the shrine, and their splendid tombs are still one of the Abbey's main attractions.

The Abbey was part of a monastery until the sixteenth century, when Henry VIII closed them all down. Today it is neither a cathedral nor a parish church but something called a 'Royal Peculiar', which means that it is directly responsible to the sovereign, not the Archbishop of Canterbury.

The Abbey is still very much a working church and it holds regular services, which visitors are welcome to attend. As well as Sunday services, evensong takes place at 17.00 during the week and at 15.00 on Saturdays. The church is also

The west front of Westminster Abbey.

On the west façade of Westminster Abbey, above the doors, are statues of ten modern martyrs, including one of Martin Luther King.

occasionally closed for special services. During visiting hours prayers are said every hour on the hour, when everyone is asked to stand quietly for a minute or two.

There is a lot to see in Westminster Abbey, so allow at least an hour for a visit. The entrance is through the north door into the north transept, more usually known as **Statesmen's Aisle** as it is crowded with monuments and statues of politicians of the eighteenth and nineteenth centuries. Among them, wearing a Roman toga, is Sir Robert Peel, who created the first proper London police force in the 1830s – his first name gave rise to the nickname 'bobby' for a policeman.

Turning left out of Statesmen's Aisle, you enter the **north ambulatory**, which has a number of chapels off to the side. To the right is the **Shrine of St Edward**, which you can see between the tombs of medieval kings and queens. It is no longer possible to go into the chapel as the ancient floor is very fragile. The shrine was once covered in gold, jewels and different coloured marbles. The recesses at the bottom are where pilgrims used to kneel to get as close as possible to the saint, hoping to be cured of their ailments. There are three royal tombs on this side: the central one is of Henry III, which has the remains of similar rich decoration; to the right is the tomb of his son Edward I, with that of Edward's wife, Eleanor of Castile, to the left. When Eleanor died in Nottinghamshire, Edward had her body brought to London. He erected a cross wherever it stopped for the night, the last one being the original Charing Cross. Round the corner, behind the shrine, is the **Coronation Chair** that Edward had made to hold the Stone of Scone on which Scottish kings had been crowned for centuries and which he stole in 1296. The chair has been used at coronations in the Abbey ever since. It looks rather battered and is covered in centuries-old graffiti, some of it carved by boys from Westminster School. In the 1950s the Stone of Scone was removed by Scottish nationalists. In 1996 it was officially returned to Scotland, where it is on display in Edinburgh Castle, but will be brought back to Westminster to be placed in the chair for all future coronations.

Steps lead up to the Lady Chapel, or **Henry VII's Chapel**, one of the most beautiful parts of the Abbey. It was built in the early sixteenth century by Henry VII in the Perpendicular style. The side chapel on the left contains the impressive **tomb of Elizabeth I**, who died in 1603. Both the tomb and her magnificent clothes and jewellery give a good idea of the splendour of the first Elizabethan era. Buried in the same tomb is her half-sister Mary I. Elizabeth and Mary were daughters of Henry VIII but were never particularly close. Mary remained a Catholic throughout her life and earned her nickname 'Bloody Mary' because of her persecution of Protestants. The Latin memorial reads: 'Consorts both in throne and grave, here rest we two sisters, Elizabeth and Mary, in the hope of one resurrection.' At the end of the chapel is **Innocents' Corner**, so called because a number of children are buried here. To left and right are the tombs of two of James I's daughters; on the left, in a cradle, is the charming figure of Sophia, who died aged only three days, while to the right is Mary, who died aged two. At the back is a small tomb said to contain the bones of the 'Princes in the Tower', Edward V and his brother Richard, who disappeared, presumed murdered, in the Tower in 1483. Some bones of children were found there in 1674 and Charles II had them buried here.

Turn left outside the side chapel through the massive gates leading into the main part of Henry VII's Chapel. The gates are decorated with many royal heraldic emblems, including Tudor roses, the English lion and a crown on a bush (a reference to the legend that the defeated Richard III's crown was found in a bush after the Battle of Bosworth, which was won by Henry VII). The whole chapel is covered in ornate decoration, including the beautiful fan-vaulted ceiling. Along both sides are the stalls of the Knights of the Bath, with the helmets and banners of today's knights above them. The Order of the Bath is the second highest order of chivalry in England and was founded by Henry IV, who made his knights wash themselves the night before his coronation. On the backs of the stalls are plates of past knights, including Lord Nelson and the Duke of Wellington. Some of the seats tip up and were originally meant to support the monks, who were able to rest on them in long services during which they were not allowed to sit down. On the underside of the seats are carvings called misericords, including a number of animals and a schoolboy having his bottom smacked. In the centre of the chapel, surrounded by railings, is the **tomb of Henry VII** and his wife, Elizabeth of York. This is one of the finest tombs in the Abbey and the bronze figures are very lifelike.

At the end of the chapel is the **RAF Memorial Chapel**, dedicated to the airmen who died in the Battle of Britain in 1940. To the left of the altar is a hole made by a bomb during the Second World War. A stone in the floor marks the place where Oliver Cromwell was buried. After the Restoration in 1660 his body was dug up and his head stuck on a pole on the roof of Westminster Hall as a traitor.

Outside the chapel to the left is another side chapel containing the magnificent **tomb of Mary, Queen of Scots**. She was imprisoned for many years and finally beheaded by her cousin, Elizabeth I, who saw her as a threat to the throne of England. Elizabeth was succeeded by Mary's son, James I, who ensured that Mary's tomb was even more splendid than Elizabeth's. Also in this chapel is the bronze effigy of Margaret Beaufort, Henry VII's mother; it has the most wonderfully wrinkled hands. Now turn left and go down the steps; to the left are more chapels and to the right the tombs of Edward III and Richard II. In 1766 a boy from Westminster School put his hand into Richard's tomb and removed the jawbone; it was not returned until 1906.

Further on is **Poets' Corner**, where many writers, musicians and actors are buried or commemorated. The first writer to be buried here was Geoffrey Chaucer, author of the *Canterbury Tales,* because he lived nearby, not because he was a poet. He was later joined by other famous writers, including Charles Dickens, the great nineteenth-century novelist, and by Handel, the composer of *Messiah*. There is a very fine monument to Shakespeare, who is buried in Stratford-upon-Avon. As so little floor space remains, recent memorials have been placed in the windows, including one to Oscar Wilde. Look out for the floor tablet to Thomas Parr, who died in 1635, apparently aged 152! The paintings on the south wall give an idea of how the Abbey once looked, as it would have been brightly painted throughout.

The area between the choir and the high altar is sometimes referred to as the **theatre**, as this is the space specially created to hold coronations. For coronations special stands are set up in the nave and transepts to seat all the extra people, and toilets and first-aid posts are brought in. The throne is set up on a platform and the Coronation Chair is placed in front of the altar. The ceremony, which lasts four hours, is performed by the Archbishop of Canterbury. The crown jewels are brought from the Tower of London, where they are normally kept. This is also where the funeral of Diana, Princess of Wales was held in September 1997.

You should now leave through the side door leading into the **cloisters**, which is where the monks used to study, teach and relax. Here you can visit the **Chapter House, Pyx Chamber and Abbey Museum**, for which there is a separate charge. The Chapter House is a beautiful octagonal room dating from the thirteenth century. There are still remains of the original paintings on the walls. The tiled floor is also original – look out for the coat of arms with the three lions and the centaur (half-man, half-horse). This was the meeting room of the Abbey and the monks would gather here every morning to discuss the business of the day. During the fourteenth century the House of Commons met here, much to the annoyance of the monks. Next door is the small Pyx Chamber, where the royal treasury was once housed. After a theft in 1303 the great wooden doors were added for greater security. Each door has three locks; for extra safety, a different person looked after each key.

The Abbey Museum next door is in part of the original abbey buildings, underneath the monks' dormitory. It houses an exhibition of funeral effigies and is a sort of Madame Tussaud's in miniature. In the Middle Ages a life-size wooden effigy of the king or queen, dressed in coronation robes, was placed on the coffin during the funeral procession. The oldest one is of Edward III and it is thought to have been taken from a death mask as it shows signs of the drooping mouth caused by the stroke which killed him. During restoration work it was found that the eyebrows were made of dog hair. From the seventeenth century a crown was placed on the coffin instead, but wax effigies were still made. They were placed next to the tomb after the funeral as a sort of tourist attraction. The effigy of Charles II is particularly fine; it is dressed in his own robes of the Order of the Garter. Another famous figure is that of Frances Stuart, Duchess of Richmond, who is dressed in the robes she wore for the coronation of Queen Anne. Next to her is her pet parrot, which died a few days after its mistress and is said to be the oldest stuffed bird in England. In a separate case is the figure of Lord Nelson, who died at the Battle of Trafalgar in 1805. Although Nelson was buried in St Paul's Cathedral, this effigy was commissioned to attract people to the Abbey. The figure is an

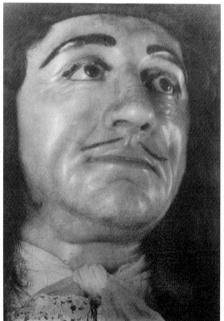

This wax effigy of King Charles II can be seen in Westminster Abbey Museum.

excellent likeness and is dressed in Nelson's own clothes, with his many decorations embroidered on the coat.

From the cloisters return to the church by another door which takes you back into the nave. You can now appreciate the great height of the building and, standing by the west door, you can look down the full length of the church. Just inside the west door, surrounded by red poppies, is the **tomb of the Unknown Warrior**, which commemorates the many thousands of soldiers who died on the French and Belgian battlefields during the First World War. The idea for the tomb was suggested by the Reverend David Railton, a chaplain in the war who had seen a simple grave in France with the inscription 'An Unknown British Soldier'. The burial took place here on 11th November 1920, two years to the day after the end of the war, and was attended by King George V. The coffin is of English oak, the soil is French and the marble Belgian. On a nearby pillar is the American Congressional Medal, the highest honour that can be conferred in the USA, bestowed upon the Unknown Warrior in 1921. There is also a simple memorial to **Sir Winston Churchill**, who was Prime Minister during the Second World War. (His funeral took place in St Paul's Cathedral and he is buried at Bladon in Oxfordshire.)

In the centre of the nave is buried **David Livingstone**, the famous missionary and explorer. He spent much of his life in Africa trying to convert the inhabitants and opening up the continent for trade. On one occasion he was gone for so long that Henry Stanley was sent to look for him. When Stanley found him he uttered the famous words 'Doctor Livingstone, I presume'. Livingstone died in Africa in 1873; his body was dried out in the sun and, disguised as a bale of cloth, was carried for nine months by his servants before being shipped back to England.

On the left-hand side of the choir screen is a memorial to the famous eighteenth-century scientist Sir Isaac Newton, who is buried in front of it. He is best known for formulating the law of gravity, suggested to him by an apple falling on his head, but he was also an important mathematician and astronomer, which is why cherubs are shown playing with scientific instruments. Around him is what is known as **Scientists' Corner**, with tombs and memorials of several other important scientists, including Charles Darwin, who developed the theory of evolution.

On the west façade of the Abbey, above the doors, are ten modern statues, unveiled in 1998. They are of twentieth-century martyrs, including Oscar Romero, the Archbishop of El Salvador assassinated in 1980, and Martin Luther King, the American civil rights campaigner killed in 1969.

WESTMINSTER ABBEY, 20 Dean's Yard, London SW1P 3PA.

Telephone: 020 7222 7110.

Website: www.westminster-abbey.org

Open: Monday to Friday 9.00–16.45, Saturday 9.00–14.45. Also Wednesday 18.00–19.45. Sometimes closed for special services.

Admission charge.

Chapter House, Pyx Chamber and Abbey Museum open April to October, daily 10.00–17.30; November to March, daily 10.00–16.00.

Admission charge.

Nearest Underground: Westminster.

Buses: 3, 11, 12, 24, 53, 77A, 88, 159, 211.

4
The Houses of Parliament

The Houses of Parliament, with the famous clock tower, is one of London's best-known landmarks. Despite its medieval style, most of the present structure was built in the nineteenth century. Edward the Confessor built his palace here in the eleventh century and it was the main royal residence until the time of Henry VIII, which is why its official name is still the Palace of Westminster. The old palace burnt down in 1834 and a competition was held for a new parliament building. The rules stated that it had to be in the Gothic style to blend in with nearby Westminster Abbey and Westminster Hall, the only part of the palace to survive the fire. The winning design was by Charles Barry. Construction began in 1839 and took over twenty years to complete. The building contains more than a thousand rooms and a hundred staircases and has 2 miles (3.2 km) of corridors.

One of the best views of the Houses of Parliament is from the middle of Westminster Bridge. From here you can see the whole of the river front, complete with a terrace where Members of Parliament can sometimes be seen relaxing. There is also a good view of the famous clock tower commonly known as **Big Ben**. In fact, Big Ben is the 13.5 ton bell which chimes the hours. It was named after either Sir Benjamin Hall, who was in charge of the building works, or a popular prizefighter of the time called Benjamin Caunt. The bell cracked soon after it was hung and this is what gives it its unique sound. The clock faces are 23 feet (7 metres) across and the minute hands are 14 feet (4.2 metres) long. It is still one of the most accurate clocks in the world; it is wound and checked three times a week and adjustments to the mechanism are still made using old pennies. If a light is on at the top of the tower at night, it means that Parliament is still sitting.

Now walk back over the bridge, past the base of Big Ben and turn left into Parliament Square. To the left is New Palace Yard. You may see MPs going in and out of the gate, which is always guarded by a policeman, as the House of Commons is at this end of the building. The next building on the left is **Westminster Hall**, which is the oldest part of the complex. In front of it is a statue of Oliver Cromwell,

The Houses of Parliament and Big Ben.

who signed Charles I's death warrant. If you turn round and look at St Margaret's Church you will see a bust of Charles I looking across at Cromwell.

At the end of Westminster Hall is St Stephen's Entrance. This is where you queue if you want to attend a debate (see below). The equestrian statue is of Richard I, the Lionheart, the popular twelfth-century king who spent most of his reign fighting in the Crusades in the Holy Land. The doorway beyond is the Peers' Entrance, as at this end of the building is the House of Lords, where unelected hereditary and life peers sit to debate bills passed to it by the Commons. The square **Victoria Tower** holds the records of Parliament, some dating back to the fifteenth century. When the Queen opens Parliament she drives in under the tower in the State Coach.

On the other side of the road is the **Jewel Tower**, which was part of Edward III's palace and was where he kept his jewels and other valuables. The gardens are regularly seen in television news broadcasts as politicians are often interviewed there on important matters of the day.

If you have arranged a guided tour of Parliament the way in is under the Victoria Tower. The tour takes you to the Queen's Robing Room, where the Queen dons her robes and crown before the State Opening of Parliament. You then walk the route she takes down the Royal Gallery, which is lined with royal portraits and two enormous paintings of the battles of Trafalgar and Waterloo, and on into the Prince's Chamber, with its marble statue of Queen Victoria. Next comes the **House of Lords**, a highly decorated chamber with historical paintings on the walls and lots of gilding. At one end is the throne, under an ornate canopy, from which the Queen addresses Parliament at the State Opening. In front of the throne is the Woolsack, the seat of the Lord Chancellor, the Speaker of the Lords, who controls debates. The name 'Woolsack' is a reminder of the time when wool was one of Britain's most precious commodities.

The route leads on to the Central Lobby, which is the meeting area for the two Houses and for anyone wishing to speak to, or 'lobby', their MP. The **House of Commons** is very much plainer than the Lords, with simple wood panelling and green benches on either side of the Speaker's chair. There are 659 elected MPs, but there is only room for 427, which is why so many of them have to stand during important debates. Following tradition, there are red lines on the floor in front of the government and opposition benches; these are two sword-lengths apart, an attempt in past centuries to prevent any fighting.

The visit ends in the vast space of the medieval **Westminster Hall**, built in the twelfth century by William II as the banqueting hall of his palace, with the wonderful wooden roof added in the fourteenth century by Richard II. The hall served as Britain's main law courts until 1882, when they moved to a new building in the Strand. Many important trials were held here, including those of Ann Boleyn, Charles I and Guy Fawkes, who attempted to blow up the king and Parliament in 1605.

To attend a debate you should queue at St Stephen's Entrance. For the House of Commons the head of the queue is usually let in at 16.15 on Monday to Thursday and 11.30 on Friday. For the Lords the time is 14.30. Group tours can be arranged by contacting your MP.

During the summer recess (August and September) guided tours are run but need to be booked at least five days in advance by telephoning 020 7344 9966. There is a small charge for these tours. School groups should contact the Education Unit on 020 7219 2105.

HOUSES OF PARLIAMENT, London SW1A 1AA.

Website: www.parliament.uk

Nearest Underground: Westminster.

Buses: 3, 11, 12, 24, 53, 77A, 88, 159, 211.

5
Whitehall walk

The short walk from Parliament Square to Trafalgar Square has lots of interesting things to see: the area is the centre of government and there are many royal associations too. The nearest Underground station to the start of the walk is Westminster.

Parliament Square is surrounded by important buildings, including Westminster Abbey and the Houses of Parliament (see Chapters 3 and 4). Because of the traffic, it is difficult to get to the grassed area in the middle, which has statues of important statesmen round the edges. The most impressive statue, opposite Big Ben, is of **Sir Winston Churchill**, who was Prime Minister during the Second World War. He is shown in a military overcoat walking with the aid of a stick towards the House of Commons, where he spent so much of his working life. Turn into Parliament Street, which later becomes **Whitehall** – the political heart of the country, with government offices lining both sides of the road. The first one on the left is the Treasury, the office of the Chancellor of the Exchequer, and beyond it is the Foreign Office.

Turn left between the two buildings, walk down King Charles Street and go down the steps at the end. On the left you will see the sand-bagged entrance to the underground **Cabinet War Rooms**, which were used by Churchill and his War Cabinet during the Second World War. The rooms were created in the basement of government offices and conditions must have been very unpleasant for those working or living here. You can visit twenty-one of the rooms and everything is authentic, including the gas-masks, newspapers and magazines which have been left lying around as if the staff have just left. All visitors are offered a free taped sound guide, which is very informative. The Cabinet Room is where the Prime Minister met with his ministers and advisers over one hundred times during the war. You will also see the tiny Transatlantic Telephone Room, which is where Churchill, using a special scrambling device, could speak directly to President Roosevelt in the USA. The door was taken from a toilet and the room was so secret that many people thought it was Churchill's private lavatory. Churchill's own room can also be seen, along with the equipment the BBC used to broadcast his speeches. In the centre of the Map Room are desks covered in different coloured telephones where officers would receive news on the progress of the war; the information was then plotted on the maps which line the walls.

CABINET WAR ROOMS, Clive Steps, King Charles Street, London SW1A 2AQ.

Telephone: 020 7930 6961. Fax: 020 7839 5897.

Website: www.iwm.org.uk

Open: April to September, daily 9.30–18.00; October to March, daily 10.00–18.00.

Admission charge.

Nearest Underground: Westminster, St James's Park.

Buses: 3, 11, 12, 24, 53, 77A, 88, 159, 211.

From the Cabinet War Rooms return to Whitehall and turn left. In the middle of the road is the **Cenotaph**, which commemorates the dead of the two world wars.

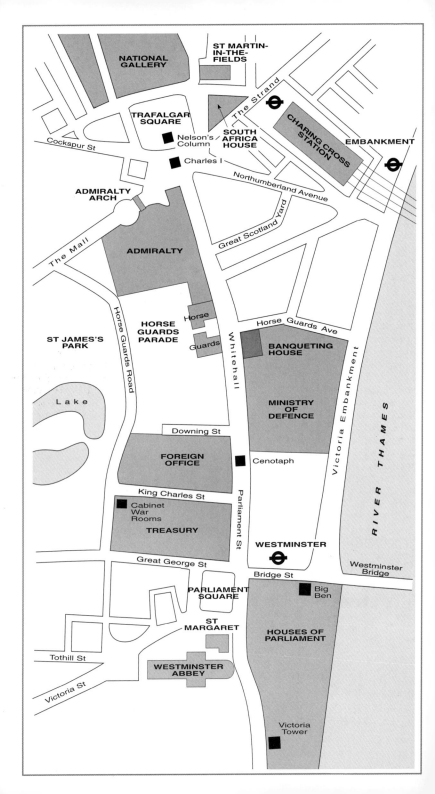

The word means 'empty tomb', and you may notice that there are no religious symbols on it. The only decoration is the flags of the Army, Royal Air Force, Royal Navy and Merchant Navy. Every year, at 11.00 on the Sunday nearest to 11th November, the day the First World War ended, a moving ceremony is held here in remembrance of the fallen. After a two-minute silence the Queen and leaders of the three main political parties lay wreaths of poppies at the foot of the memorial, and there is a march-past of war veterans, who also lay wreaths in memory of lost colleagues and friends.

A little further on, on the left, is one of London's most famous addresses, **10 Downing Street**, the official residence of the Prime Minister since the eighteenth century. The street is closed off by security gates, but you can get a glimpse of Number 10 on the right; you may even be lucky enough to see the Prime Minister or Cabinet ministers coming and going through the gates in their chauffeur-driven cars. The Chancellor of the Exchequer occupies the house next door, at Number 11. The street is named after Sir George Downing, who leased the land and built the houses in the seventeenth century to sell to the well-to-do. Downing was a successful MP and diplomat but was held in low esteem by his colleagues, who considered him to be mean and dishonest, and it is unfortunate that such qualities are associated through his name with those at the heart of government.

Next on your right is a massive building with a green roof. This is the **Ministry of Defence**, and on the lawns in front of it are statues of three commanders from the Second World War: Field Marshals Slim, Alanbrooke and Montgomery, who was affectionately known as 'Monty'. The smaller statue is of Sir Walter Raleigh, the Elizabethan explorer who introduced potatoes and tobacco to England from the New World.

Not far beyond, also on the right, is the **Banqueting House**, the only remaining part of the old Palace of Whitehall that burnt down in 1698. It was built in 1619 for James I to host important functions and its classical style and use of stone would have been very modern and impressive at a time when most buildings were made of brick. James's son, Charles I, later commissioned the famous Flemish artist Rubens to paint the magnificent ceiling, which glorified his father and the Stuart dynasty. By a cruel irony, only a few years later on a cold day in January 1649 Charles stepped out of one of the windows of the building on the way to his execution. He wore an extra shirt so that he would not shiver and be thought to be afraid.

Trafalgar Square and the National Gallery.

25

BANQUETING HOUSE, Whitehall, London SW1A 2ER.

Telephone: 020 7930 4179.

Website: www.hrp.org.uk

Open: Monday to Saturday 10.00–17.00. Sometimes closed at short notice for functions.

Admission charge.

Nearest Underground: Westminster, Charing Cross.

Buses: 3, 11, 12, 24, 53, 77A, 88, 159, 211.

On the other side of Whitehall from the Banqueting House is **Horse Guards**, usually with two mounted guards in front. This is the official entrance to Buckingham Palace. It is guarded by the Household Cavalry, which consists of two regiments: the Life Guards, who wear red tunics and have white plumes in their helmets, and the Blues and Royals, with blue tunics and red plumes. They are relieved every hour but at 11.00 (10.00 on Sundays) the Guard is changed in a brief but colourful ceremony. Through the arch is Horse Guards Parade, where the Trooping the Colour ceremony takes places in June to celebrate the Sovereign's official birthday (see Chapter 1). If you take a close look at the clock over the archway you will notice a black mark by the number 2. This is a reminder of the hour when Charles I was beheaded in 1649 outside the Banqueting House opposite.

Now continue up Whitehall and on the left, behind a screen with seahorses on top, is the **Admiralty**. It was here that the body of Admiral Nelson lay in state after it had been brought back from the Battle of Trafalgar in 1805. Ahead of you is **Trafalgar Square**, created to commemorate the victory. In the middle of the square is Nelson's Column, with a statue of the great naval hero on top. The height of the whole monument is 170 feet (52 metres) and the statue is 17 feet (5.2 metres) high. Shortly before the statue of Nelson was put up in 1843 fourteen people ate dinner on top of the column! The reliefs around the base are made from captured French cannon and depict scenes from four of Nelson's victories. Around the column are Landseer's famous lions, popular with children, who love to clamber over them. The square is also famous for its pigeons, though they are now considered to be a health risk and you can no longer buy bird seed to feed them. The square is the venue for many rallies and demonstrations throughout the year. Every December the square is dominated by a Christmas tree given by the city of Oslo as a mark of gratitude for the help given to Norway during the Second World War, and on New Year's Eve people traditionally gather here to welcome in the New Year, though this is not recommended for families because of the size of the crowds.

In the centre of the wall on the north side of the square are the Imperial Standards of Length, with the official lengths of the inch, foot and yard, a useful reminder in these days of metrication. Beyond, and filling the whole of the north side of the square, is the **National Gallery**, one of the world's great art galleries (see Chapter 7).

On the south side of the square is the equestrian **statue of Charles I**, looking down towards the site of his execution. There is a curious story attached to the statue: after Charles's execution a man called Rivett bought the statue and claimed to have melted it down to sell souvenirs made from the metal, although he had actually buried it in his garden; when Charles II was restored to the throne the statue was dug up and placed here. A plaque on the ground in front of the statue marks the centre of London, and it is from here that all distances to other towns and cities are measured.

Over to the right is **Admiralty Arch**, with its three round arches. It was erected as a memorial to Queen Victoria and forms the entrance to the Mall, which leads to Buckingham Palace (see Chapter 8). On the opposite side of the square you will see what was once Britain's smallest police station, set inside a lamp standard (though it seems to be used now as a broom cupboard). Behind it is **South Africa House**, with a golden springbok on the corner of the building. It was from the balcony facing the square that Nelson Mandela addressed a huge crowd during his visit in 1996.

The church overlooking the square is **St Martin-in-the-Fields**, the parish church of Buckingham Palace; all baptisms in the palace are entered in the church registers. Over the entrance is the coat of arms of George I, who was the first churchwarden of the church. After the First World War the crypt was used to house homeless soldiers back from the war and today the church continues to work with London's homeless and is kept warm for them to come in off the streets. In Duncannon Street is the entrance to the crypt, where you will find the **London Brass Rubbing Centre**. Here you can make rubbings of replica brasses or buy ready-made copies. It is easy and fun, and a rubbing makes an unusual souvenir.

ST MARTIN-IN-THE FIELDS, Trafalgar Square, London WC2N 4JJ.

Telephone: 020 7766 1100.

Website: www.stmartin-in-the-fields.org

Church open daily from 8.00. Crypt open Monday to Saturday 10.00–20.00, Sunday 12.00–18.00.

LONDON BRASS RUBBING CENTRE, St Martin-in-the-Fields Church, Trafalgar Square, London WC2N 4JJ.

Telephone/fax: 020 7930 9306.

Open: Monday to Saturday 10.00–18.00; Sunday 12.00–18.00. Charge for materials.

Nearest Underground: Charing Cross, Leicester Square.

Buses: 3, 6, 9, 11, 12, 13, 15, 23, 24, 29, 53, 77A, 88, 91, 139, 159, 176.

6
The National Portrait Gallery

The National Portrait Gallery is in St Martin's Place, just around the corner from the National Gallery. It houses an extensive collection of portraits of famous British men and women from all walks of life from the Middle Ages to the present day. As well as paintings there are drawings, sculpture and photographs. You can find out what Britain's great and good looked like, but the pictures are also a wonderful visual panorama of changing fashions in clothes and hairstyles. You also get to see the different image kings, queens and politicians through the centuries wished to project, from the stiff, formal early portraits to the greater informality of recent years. There is an excellent sound guide which gives an interesting commentary on nearly two hundred of the pictures, bringing them alive with archive recordings of people such as Churchill, Baden-Powell and Florence Nightingale.

The gallery was refurbished in 2000, with new gallery space added and a restaurant on the top floor which offers stunning views of Nelson's Column, Whitehall and beyond. Start by going to the information desk to pick up a plan of the galleries so you can choose where you want to start. If you want to visit in chronological order, take the escalator up to the second floor to the Tudor galleries and work down the building. Alternatively, if you want to select a few pictures to look at you could visit the **IT Gallery** to the right of the escalator. Here you can use one of the touch-screen computers to look through the collection and print out your

The Tudor galleries at the National Portrait Gallery.

own personalised tour.

In the **Tudor galleries** you will find Holbein's life-size drawing of Henry VIII, showing him in a typically robust pose, with legs apart and hands on hips. There is also a curious distorted portrait of his son, Edward VI, which has to be viewed through a peephole at the side to make any sense. There are three dazzling images of Elizabeth I, dressed to kill in her fine clothes and draped with expensive jewels, and she is surrounded by many of her courtiers, including Francis Drake and Walter Raleigh. Also here is the only portrait of Shakespeare made during his lifetime.

In the **Stuart galleries** are portraits of the diarist Samuel Pepys and Henry Purcell, Britain's first great composer. Charles II is here with his wife, Catherine of Braganza, along with several of his mistresses, including Nell Gwyn in a very revealing dress. Side by side in another room are portraits of Lord Nelson and Lady Hamilton, whose relationship was one of history's great love affairs, although it scandalised many people at the time.

The **Victorian age** is very well represented, with Queen Victoria and her consort, Prince Albert, along with plenty of politicians, writers, scientists and artists. Here is the triple portrait of the three Brontë sisters by their brother Branwell, and the artist Landseer modelling the famous lions of Trafalgar Square. On the first-floor landing is a display of portraits of the present royal family. The displays covering the twentieth century to the present day include images not only of writers and politicians but also of actors and sportsmen, and the display is constantly being updated.

NATIONAL PORTRAIT GALLERY, St Martin's Place, London WC2H 0HE.
Telephone: 020 7306 0055. Fax: 020 7306 0056.
Website: www.npg.org.uk
Open: Saturday to Wednesday 10.00–18.00; Thursday and Friday 10.00–21.00.
Admission free, except for special exhibitions.
Nearest Underground: Charing Cross, Leicester Square, Piccadilly Circus.
Buses: 3, 6, 9, 11, 12, 13, 15, 23, 24, 29, 53, 77A, 88, 91, 139, 159, 176.

7
The National Gallery

The National Gallery is one of the world's great art galleries, containing many masterpieces of European art from the thirteenth century to about 1900, including important works by Raphael, Leonardo da Vinci, Rembrandt, Monet, Renoir and Van Gogh. The gallery was founded in 1824 with only thirty-eight pictures when the collection of John Julius Angerstein was bought for the nation; there are now over two thousand on display. It would take many visits to see all the paintings, so it is best not to do too much at once. You can pick up a free map of the gallery from the information desk, listing the major artists to be found in each room.

The Education Department offers free gallery talks to school groups from Britain which can be tailored to any particular requirements you may have. You might like to try the *Gallery Guide Soundtrack*, a CD-Rom guide to almost every picture in the gallery. The commentary is informative and not too technical, so it is suitable for older children as well as adults. Quizzes and activity booklets are available for younger children from the information desks. In the Sainsbury Wing is the Micro Gallery, a computerised information system with background details on all the pictures in the gallery.

To visit the gallery in chronological order, start in the modern **Sainsbury Wing**, where the oldest pictures are on display. Many of the early pictures are religious altarpieces, including the *Wilton Diptych*, a small two-panel painting showing Richard II being presented to the Christ Child. It is very decorative, with lots of rich gold leaf, and the bright blue is made of the semi-precious stone lapis lazuli, which in those days was even more expensive than gold. Notice that the angels all wear Richard's personal emblem, the white hart, which is also on the back of the picture, and this suggests the picture was probably made for the king. One of the most

A young artist seeking inspiration at the National Gallery.

popular pictures in the gallery is Van Eyck's *Arnolfini Portrait*. Van Eyck was famous for his amazingly lifelike detail, and he must have used a very fine brush to have painted every single hair of the little dog. The lady looks to modern eyes as if she is pregnant, but this was simply the fashionable look of the time. Look out for the painting by the Spanish artist Bermejo of *St Michael Triumphant over the Devil.* St Michael in his gleaming armour is about to slay a most impressive Devil, with flaming red eyes, two gaping mouths and snakes slithering out from between the vicious teeth.

Moving into the **main building**, you will find several portraits by the German artist Holbein, court painter to Henry VIII. *The Ambassadors* shows his skill at creating realistic likenesses, but it also has a hidden meaning in the odd-looking shape in the foreground. When looked at from the right-hand side it turns out to be a skull, a reminder that, however rich or powerful we might be, we must all die. A very unusual portrait entitled *A Grotesque Old Woman* shows someone wearing a very curious head-dress, who may look familiar: she was the inspiration for Tenniel's drawing of the Ugly Duchess in *Alice in Wonderland.* There are a number of pictures by the important Dutch artist Rembrandt, including two self-portraits and the dramatic *Belshazzar's Feast*, in which Belshazzar is the only one who sees the 'writing on the wall' foretelling his death while the baffled party-goers look on. You will also find many fine paintings by the great Flemish artist Rubens, including the charming portrait of *Susannah Lunden*, with her large, dark eyes, and some impressive portraits by Van Dyck, including his *Equestrian Portrait of Charles I*. Charles was less than 5 feet (1.5 metres) tall, but the artist makes him look very regal astride the splendid horse. One of the most dramatic paintings in the gallery is Caravaggio's *Supper at Emmaus*, showing the moment when two disciples recognised Jesus as he broke the bread. The artist was famous for his extreme realism; elbows and hands seem to come right out of the picture, and the bowl of fruit looks as if it is about to fall off the table on to the floor in front of you.

The gallery has a very good collection of **English pictures** from the eighteenth and early nineteenth centuries, including many portraits. Hogarth's *The Graham Children* is a particularly charming group portrait, with the boy playing a musical instrument and the baby in a curious kind of cart. Look for the wonderfully lively cat, which is taking great interest in the terrified bird in the cage. If you like horses you cannot fail to be impressed by Stubbs's dramatic life-size portrait of a famous racehorse, *Whistlejacket*. It is so lifelike that while the artist was working on it Whistlejacket attacked the painting, thinking it was another horse. Wright of Derby's *Experiment with an Air Pump* shows a travelling showman demonstrating a vacuum with the use of a rather exotic cockatoo, which looks as if it is dying from lack of oxygen. The spectators all display different emotions; one girl looks particularly upset at the plight of the poor bird, though it would not have come to any harm. Constable is renowned for his English landscapes and *The Hay Wain* is probably his most famous – its tranquil scene has been reproduced on biscuit tins and table mats many times over. What may be surprising is that it was heavily criticised when first shown in England and that for most of his life Constable was not recognised as the great artist he was. Turner was much more successful in his lifetime. *The Fighting Téméraire* shows his fascination with ships and dramatic sunsets; the ship that once fought at the Battle of Trafalgar, its useful life now over, is shown on the way up the Thames to be broken up.

There is nearly always a crowd in front of *The Execution of Lady Jane Grey* by the nineteenth-century French artist Paul Delaroche. It is a highly theatrical scene, with the young queen kneeling blindfolded before the block in the Tower of London, and the executioner standing by with his axe. The painting is very realistic, almost photographic, though not historically accurate, as she was actually executed in the open air.

The last few rooms in the gallery contain a wonderful collection of pictures by all

A group of children enjoy a talk at the National Gallery.

the most important **Impressionist** and **Post-Impressionist** artists. Monet visited London several times, and his *Thames below Westminster* is a typically misty view of the then very modern Houses of Parliament. Renoir's *Boating on the Seine* shows two women enjoying a hot summer's day on the river and was mostly painted outdoors, something the Impressionists were famous for. One of the best-known pictures in the gallery is Van Gogh's *Sunflowers*, a riot of different yellows, with paint sometimes so thick the flowers look almost real. One of the most delightful pictures in the whole gallery is Henri Rousseau's *Tiger in a Tropical Storm (Surprised)*, which shows a tiger running through the jungle in a torrential downpour. Rousseau did not train as an artist and gave up his job as a gatekeeper to paint, but his rather primitive style is what gives his pictures their charm. Although he painted many jungle pictures he had probably never been anywhere near a jungle: he studied plants in a botanical garden and even used common household plants and simply made them larger than normal, like the rubber plant in the right foreground.

NATIONAL GALLERY, Trafalgar Square, London WC2N 5DN.
Telephone: 020 7747 2885 (Education Department: 020 7747 2424).
Website: www.nationalgallery.org.uk
Open: daily 10.00–18.00 (Wednesday until 21.00).
Admission free, except for special exhibitions.
Nearest Underground: Leicester Square, Charing Cross, Piccadilly Circus.
Buses: 3, 6, 9, 11, 12, 13, 15, 23, 24, 29, 53, 77A, 88, 91, 139, 159, 176.

8
Around Buckingham Palace

The best way to approach Buckingham Palace is to walk from Trafalgar Square through Admiralty Arch into the Mall, giving you the long vista all the way up to the front of the palace. The road is painted red as it is used as a processional route for important royal ceremonies such as Trooping the Colour, royal weddings, the State Opening of Parliament and state visits. On the right is the impressive white Carlton House Terrace, which houses the Institute of Contemporary Arts where modern art exhibitions are held. Just past the ICA, up some steps on the right, is the **Duke of York's Column**, a memorial to Frederick, the second son of George III. He was commander-in-chief of the Army and his supposed lack of leadership inspired the nursery rhyme 'The Grand Old Duke of York', in which he marches his men to the top of the hill, then marches them down again. In reality he was popular with his men, and the memorial was paid for by stopping one day's pay from every soldier in the army.

Up the left-hand side of the Mall is **St James's Park**, one of London's loveliest Royal Parks and a good spot for a picnic at the end of the walk. There are lots of colourful flowerbeds and the lake is full of interesting birds, from common British ducks to the more exotic Australian black swans and the famous pelicans, which have been kept here since the days of Charles II. During the summer there are concerts in the bandstand to the north of the lake. From the bridge over the lake there are fine views towards Buckingham Palace in one direction and Horse Guards and Whitehall in the other.

Continue on down the Mall past the red and white **Marlborough House**, built by Sir Christopher Wren, the architect of St Paul's Cathedral. Further on, past Marlborough Road, is the back of **St James's Palace**, a royal palace not open to the public, as members of the royal family, including Prince Charles, have apartments

Feeding the ducks in St James's Park.

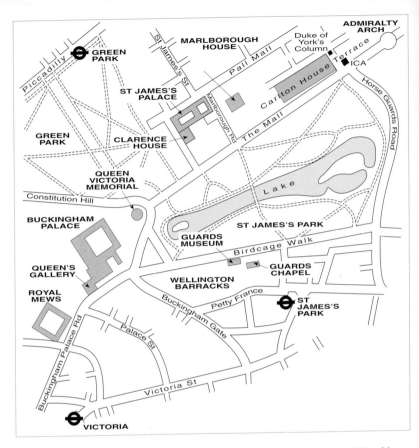

there. It was built by Henry VIII and from the seventeenth century until Buckingham Palace was built in the nineteenth century was the main royal residence. For a view of the original Tudor gateway, which is guarded by foot soldiers, turn left at the end of Marlborough Road. In Marlborough Road itself is **Friary Court**, where the Old Guard, complete with its band, assembles at 11.00 before setting off at 11.15 to march down to change the guard at Buckingham Palace. After the ceremony the New Guard marches back up the Mall and arrives a little after 12.00. If you like to avoid crowds, this is a good spot to enjoy a bit of pageantry without encountering the large numbers of people at Buckingham Palace which make it very hard to see anything. Return to the Mall and turn right. The cream building on the right is **Clarence House**, the home of the Queen Mother. A little further on to the right is **Green Park**, so called because it has no formal flowerbeds, although the grass is smothered in flowers in the spring.

By now you will have a good view of the well-known façade of **Buckingham Palace**. In front of it is the massive white **Queen Victoria Memorial**, which is a good vantage point for watching Changing the Guard. Buckingham Palace has been the official London residence of the monarch since Queen Victoria first moved there in 1837, though much of it had been built for George IV. There are over six hundred rooms, including private apartments for the Queen and her family, rooms for her staff and a series of splendid State Rooms. The Royal Standard flies from the flagpole when the Queen is at home, and the Union Flag flies at all other times.

During August and September it is possible to visit the **State Rooms** of Buckingham Palace as the Queen is not in residence. These are the rooms used for ceremonies such as investitures and to entertain important visitors, and they are laid out as they would be for these occasions. They were not made to be lived in, but to impress, and this they still manage to do. The ornate rooms are filled with antique furniture and wonderful paintings from the royal collection, including many impressive portraits. You enter through the Ambassadors' Entrance and pass through the inner quadrangle into the Grand Entrance. At the top of the spectacular Grand Staircase you enter a series of rooms leading to the Throne Room, which has a number of thrones used at coronations. It is here that the Queen receives guests on formal occasions. The Picture Gallery is hung with some of the finest paintings by artists such as Van Dyck, Rubens and Rembrandt. One of the most beautiful rooms is the Music Room, where several royal children have been christened. You can also visit the impressive Ballroom, which is no longer used for balls, but for concerts, state banquets and investitures, when honours are presented to men and women from all walks of life. At the end of the tour you leave via the gardens, where there are toilets and a souvenir shop.

BUCKINGHAM PALACE, London SW1A 1AA.

Telephone: 020 7321 2233 (credit card line). Fax: 020 7930 9625.

Group bookings: 020 7839 1377.

Website: www.royalresidences.com

Open: August to September, daily 9.30–16.30.

Admission charge.

Nearest Undergound: Victoria, St James's Park, Green Park, Hyde Park Corner.

Buses: 2, 8, 11, 16, 24, 36, 38, 52, 73, 82, 185, 211, 239, 507, C1, C10.

One of London's most popular attractions is the **Changing the Guard** ceremony, which takes place in the forecourt of Buckingham Palace at 11.30, daily in summer and every other day in winter (telephone: 09068 353718 to check). It is always very

crowded, so it is advisable to arrive early. The Old Guard from St James's Palace arrives at around 11.20 to join the Buckingham Palace Old Guard. At 11.25 the New Guard leaves Wellington Barracks in Birdcage Walk. The ceremony itself lasts about half an hour, during which all the guards are changed and the band plays throughout (the changeover from the Old to the New Guard takes place early on in the ceremony but as no key actually changes hands these days you probably will not notice it happen). At 12.05 the Old Guard returns to Wellington Barracks and part of the New Guard marches up the Mall to St James's Palace to take over their duties there.

Changing the Guard at Buckingham Palace.

To find out more about the five regiments of the Foot Guards, you might like to visit the **Guards Museum** in Wellington Barracks in Birdcage Walk. On display are uniforms, weapons and souvenirs of 350 years of military campaigns, including the Battle of Waterloo and the Falklands War, reminding us that the Guards are real soldiers, not just a colourful tourist attraction. At the end of the visit it is possible to try on a busby or bearskin. Some of them are over a hundred years old and have been handed down from father to son.

GUARDS MUSEUM, Wellington Barracks, Birdcage Walk, London SW1E 6HQ.

Telephone: 020 7414 3271.

Open: daily 10.00–16.00 (closed January and on some ceremonial days).

Admission charge.

Nearest Underground: St James's Park, Victoria.

Buses: 11, 24, 211, 507.

Along Buckingham Gate are two more parts of the palace open to the public. First is the **Queen's Gallery**, which holds changing exhibitions of items from the royal collections, including paintings, jewellery, furniture and photographs. After major refurbishment the gallery is due to reopen in 2002, when much more of the collection will be on view. A little further up the road is the **Royal Mews**, where the Queen's horses and carriages are on display. The highlight is the splendidly decorated Gold State Coach, which is used to take the monarch to and from Westminster Abbey for the coronation. There are several other carriages on display, including those used for other royal occasions such as the State Opening of Parliament, state visits and royal weddings. The newest is the Australian State Coach, presented to the Queen in 1988 as a gift from the Australian people. Also on display are a number of miniature carriages made for royal children. You can visit the stables where the carriage horses are housed and where there are also displays of harnesses and saddles.

ROYAL MEWS, Buckingham Palace Road, London SW1A 1AA.

Telephone: 020 7321 2233.

Website: www.royalresidences.com

Open: October to July, Monday to Thursday 12.00–16.00; August to September, Monday to Thursday 10.30–16.30.

Admission charge.

Nearest Underground: Victoria.

Buses: 2, 8, 11, 16, 24, 36, 38, 52, 73, 82, 185, 211, 239, 507, C1, C10.

9
The West End

The West End of London is famous for its shops, cinemas, theatres and restaurants. It was the area to which the well-to-do moved when the old part of London in and around the city walls became overcrowded and it has always been more prosperous than the East End. The heart of the West End is generally considered to be Piccadilly Circus. This chapter contains several walks all starting from there. Within a short distance of Piccadilly Circus you will find some of London's best-known department stores and toyshops, a huge choice of restaurants offering a variety of food from all around the world, cinemas showing all the latest movies, and theatres offering a wide range of high quality shows.

Piccadilly Circus is one of London's busiest road junctions (six major roads lead off from it) and it is always full of people, either rushing somewhere else or just watching the world go by. On the south side is the famous statue of **Eros**, still shooting his arrows from the top of a fountain. The statue is not in fact of the Greek god of love but represents the Angel of Christian Charity and is a memorial to the Earl of Shaftesbury, the nineteenth-century social reformer who put a stop to young children working in the coal mines. The Circus is continuously lit up by colourful neon lights advertising many famous names and is particularly impressive at night – notice the computerised Coca-Cola sign with its constantly changing images. On the corner of Haymarket is a dramatic fountain called the Horses of Helios.

Overlooking the Circus is the London Pavilion, once a cinema, but now home to **Rock Circus**, a celebration of rock and pop music from the 1950s to the present day. There are wax models of famous rock stars from Elvis Presley and the Beatles to Michael Jackson, Madonna and the Spice Girls, with speakers playing their greatest hits. Also on display are memorabilia such as suits worn by the Beatles and a pair of

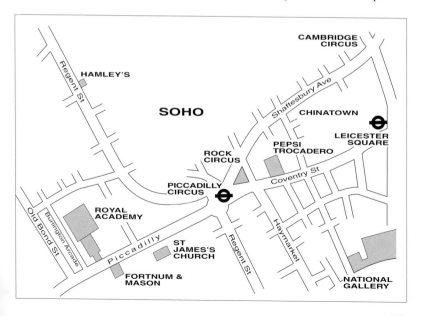

The real Spice Girls with their life-size models in Rock Circus.

Elton John's platform shoes. The Graveyard Zone commemorates dead stars such as John Lennon, Marc Bolan and Freddie Mercury.

ROCK CIRCUS, The London Pavilion, 1 Piccadilly Circus, London W1V 9LA.
Telephone: 020 7734 7203. Fax: 020 7734 8023.
Website: www.rock-circus.com
Open: daily 10.00–17.30 (Monday and Tuesday from 11.00).
Admission charge.
Nearest Underground: Piccadilly Circus.
Buses: 3, 6, 9, 12, 13, 14, 15, 19, 22, 23, 38, 53, 88, 94, 139, 159.

Piccadilly stretches from Piccadilly Circus to Hyde Park Corner. The unusual name comes from Piccadilly Hall, the house of a man who made his fortune in the seventeenth century making lace collars called 'piccadils'. A short way along Piccadilly on the left is Waterstone's, the biggest bookshop in London. Further along on the same side is **St James's Church**, built by Sir Christopher Wren. It was rebuilt after being badly damaged in the Second World War. The spire is made of fibreglass but looks like copper. Lunchtime concerts are often held in the church. In the courtyard is a cafe open seven days a week, and a craft market operates from Wednesday to Saturday. Further along on the left is one of London's most famous shops, **Fortnum & Mason**, a department store used by the royal family, as you can see from the royal coats of arms over the door. It is particularly noted for its food hall on the ground floor and for the fact that you may be served by men wearing old-fashioned tail coats. Mr Fortnum was a footman to George III and began his business by selling half-burned royal candles to members of the Court. Every hour on the hour Mr Fortnum and Mr Mason can be seen appearing from the mechanical clock over the entrance and bowing to each other.

On the other side of Piccadilly, through an archway, is the **Royal Academy**, where art exhibitions are held regularly. In the courtyard is a statue of its first president, the famous portrait painter Sir Joshua Reynolds, who wears a coloured sash during the annual Summer Exhibition.

ROYAL ACADEMY, Burlington House, Piccadilly, London W1V 0DS.
Telephone: 020 7300 8000.
Website: www.royalacademy.org.uk
Open: 10.00–18.00 (Friday 10.00–20.00).
Admission charge.
Nearest Underground: Green Park, Piccadilly Circus.
Buses: 8, 9, 14, 19, 22, 38.

To the left of the Royal Academy is **Burlington Arcade**, lined with elegant, fashionable shops. Originally built to stop people throwing their rubbish over the wall into Lord Cavendish's garden, it is guarded by uniformed beadles whose job is to make sure people comply with the rules against running, singing and carrying large parcels.

Further along on the right is **Bond Street**, home to many fashionable shops, including designer boutiques, jewellers and art galleries. A little way up on the right is one of London's more unusual statues: Winston Churchill, complete with cigar, and President Roosevelt chatting on a bench. There is room for you to sit with them and have your photograph taken!

Curving away north from Piccadilly Circus is **Regent Street**, famous for its many shops such as the department stores Liberty and Dickins & Jones. The street was originally designed by John Nash for the Prince Regent (later George IV), who

Hamleys, the famous toy shop in Regent Street.

wanted a new street to run from his palace overlooking St James's Park to what is now Regent's Park.

On the right-hand side are two shops popular with children of all ages. First is the **Disney Store**, which sells themed merchandise and clothing based on all the famous Disney characters and films. Further up the street is probably the most famous toyshop of them all, **Hamleys**. Its seven floors offer everything from traditional toys, such as dolls and teddy bears, to magic tricks and computer games. Even if you can resist the temptation to buy something, a visit is always fun, as members of staff demonstrate many of the products. The original store, known as 'Noah's Ark', opened in 1760 in High Holborn; it moved to Regent Street in 1906.

Also leading from Piccadilly Circus, **Shaftesbury Avenue** is lined with shops, restaurants and several major theatres. On the right is the Rainforest Cafe, where your meal will probably be interrupted by animatronic gorillas and tropical storms. Streets off to the left lead into the heart of **Soho**. Despite its seedy image it is full of interesting small shops and a cosmopolitan selection of restaurants and cafes, some of which spill on to the pavement.

You will probably already have noticed a lot of Chinese shops and restaurants in the area, as we are now near **Chinatown**, a part of Soho that has been taken over by the Chinese community. Turn right down Wardour Street and left into Gerrard Street and you will discover through a huge decorated archway a lively pedestrianised street lined with Chinese restaurants and supermarkets. The street names are in English and Chinese, and even the telephone boxes have been specially designed to blend in. You can often hear traditional Chinese music being played. Some of the best Chinese food in London is served here, and the many restaurants offer food from all the different regions of China. Every year, in January or February, the Chinese New Year is celebrated, a colourful and noisy occasion with lion dances and music that has become a popular attraction with visitors (see Chapter 1).

Heading east from Piccadilly Circus, a little way along Coventry Street is the **Pepsi Trocadero**, which as well as shops has several floors of hi-tech attractions, including virtual reality rides and interactive games. Also part of the complex is the popular **Planet Hollywood** theme restaurant. You will soon find yourself in **Leicester Square**, famous for its cinemas showing all the latest films and the place to come to see the stars or royalty attending film premieres. There is also a good selection of restaurants. The square is completely pedestrianised and there is usually music and street theatre to be enjoyed throughout the day. (The entertainers draw large crowds and also, therefore, pickpockets.) In the centre of the square is a statue of Shakespeare and nearby is a smaller statue of Charlie Chaplin in his most famous role as the Tramp. At each entrance to the park are busts of famous people who lived nearby, including the scientist Sir Isaac Newton and the artist William Hogarth. In the pavement around the outside of the gardens are the handprints of famous film stars, such as Clint Eastwood, Michael Caine and Tom Cruise.

On the south side of the square is the **Half Price Ticket Booth**, where you can buy unsold theatre tickets at half price plus a small fee for certain shows for performances that day. You may not get tickets for the most popular shows in town, but there is always a good selection to choose from. It is open from Monday to Saturday from 12.00 to 18.30.

10
Somerset House

Overlooking both the Strand and the Thames is Somerset House, one of London's newest cultural attractions. The building is over two hundred years old, having been built in the late eighteenth century on the site of a Tudor palace of the same name. It started out as government offices and was used by the Navy Office and the Registry of Births, Deaths and Marriages; the Inland Revenue still occupies part of the building today. The central courtyard has been cleared of parked cars, allowing the public to enjoy one of London's loveliest open spaces. In the centre of the courtyard is a most unusual new fountain, with fifty-five jets coming straight out of the pavement, spaced so that people can walk in amongst them (except on windy days). The fountains operate from 10.00 until 23.00, and every half hour there is a brief computer-operated display when the jets change height to create a variety of different shapes. Longer displays take place at 13.00, 18.00 and 22.00, with the night-time show having added coloured lights. The fountain can be turned off to allow a range of popular open air events to take place. To the south of the courtyard are the Seamen's Waiting Hall and from here a corridor leads to the shop and the dramatic Nelson Stair. You can also walk out on to the River Terrace, which offers views of the Thames through the trees. From the terrace a ramp takes you on to Waterloo Bridge, giving you easy access to the attractions of the South Bank on the other side of the river (see Chapter 24).

In the north wing of Somerset House, overlooking the Strand, is the **Courtauld Gallery**, famous for its collection of Impressionist and Post-Impressionist paintings. Here you will find masterpieces by Monet, Pissarro, Gauguin and Cézanne, as well as Van Gogh's celebrated *Self-Portrait with Bandaged Ear*, painted after he tried to cut off his ear in a moment of madness. There are also a number of good eighteenth-century British portraits and a whole room of very fine paintings by Rubens. The rooms were originally created for the Royal Academy and they retain much of their original decoration, and this creates the atmosphere of a country house rather than a museum.

Two other collections are displayed in the riverside wing of Somerset House. The entrance to them is from the Victoria Embankment, through a large arch with a central carved figure of Father Thames; this was once the entrance to the building from the Thames, but the effect was lost when the Embankment was built in the 1860s. In a special gallery in the basement is a fine carved and gilded eighteenth-century Navy Commissioner's barge which would once have used this entrance. The **Gilbert Collection** was given to the nation by Sir Arthur Gilbert, a London-born millionaire based in California. It consists of a dazzling array of jewel-encrusted gold boxes, elaborate silverware, exquisite portrait miniatures and colourful mosaics. The **Hermitage Rooms** house a changing display of items from the Hermitage Museum in St Petersburg, including paintings and furniture. The rooms have been specially refurbished to look like a wing of the great Russian museum, with spectacular replicas of some of its patterned wooden floors.

SOMERSET HOUSE, Strand, London WC2R 1LA.

Telephone: 020 7845 4600.

Website: www.somerset-house.org.uk

continued overleaf

Open: Monday to Saturday, 10.00–18.00; Sunday and bank holiday Monday 12.00–18.00.

Admission charges to Courtauld Gallery, Gilbert Collection and Hermitage Rooms.

Joint ticket to Courtauld Gallery and Gilbert Collection available.

Admission free Mondays 10.00–14.00 (except bank holidays).

Highlights tours available on 020 7845 4600.

COURTAULD GALLERY
Telephone: 020 7848 2526.
Website: www.courtauld.ac.uk

GILBERT COLLECTION
Telephone: 020 7420 9400. Fax: 020 7420 9440.
Website: www.gilbert-collection.org.uk

HERMITAGE ROOMS
Tickets should be pre-booked through Ticketmaster on 020 7413 3398.
Website: www.hermitagerooms.com

Nearest Underground: Covent Garden, Charing Cross, Embankment, Holborn, Temple (closed Sunday).

Buses: 1, 4, 6, 9, 11, 13, 15, 23, 59, 68, 76, 77A, 91, 168, 171, 176, 188, 501, 521.

The central courtyard of Somerset House was used as a skating rink during Christmas 2000.

11
Covent Garden

Once a thriving market where hotels, restaurants and shops bought their fruit and vegetables, Covent Garden is now one of London's liveliest and most popular areas, with an exciting mixture of shops, market stalls, restaurants, museums and street entertainment. During the Middle Ages it was a convent garden tended by the monks of Westminster Abbey, but when Henry VIII sold off the monasteries the land passed to the Russell family. As London grew, the land became valuable and in the seventeenth century it was developed as an elegant square or, because of its Italian style, a piazza, a name it has retained. The first occupants were wealthy people looking to get away from the cramped, smelly streets of the old city, but by the eighteenth century theatres, coffee houses and a market had taken over and the aristocrats moved to newer developments in Mayfair and Bloomsbury. The market grew so much in the nineteenth century that new buildings were added and it became London's main fruit, vegetable and flower market. Because of the congestion, the market moved in 1974 to Nine Elms, south of the river, and, despite talk of knocking down all the market buildings for redevelopment, fortunately these attractive buildings were kept and restored.

Throughout the day crowds are drawn by street entertainers of all sorts, from fire-eaters, jugglers and unicyclists to mime artists and opera singers. The most popular spot is in front of the portico of **St Paul's Church**. There is a plaque on the church recording the first Punch and Judy show performed here in 1662; at weekends Punch and Judy shows are again given in the piazza. The opening scene of the popular musical *My Fair Lady* takes places under the church portico, when Professor Higgins first hears Eliza Dolittle selling her flowers in her strangled cockney accent. The church itself is known as the 'Actors' Church', as so many actors are buried or commemorated in it. The entrance is not through the portico, but in King Street, just around the corner.

As you walk through the main market building notice the pineapples on the

Street entertainers in Covent Garden.

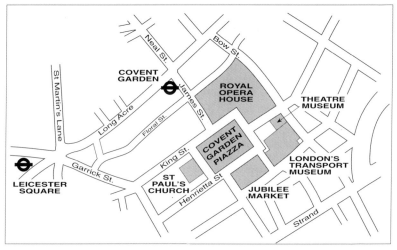

lamps, a reminder that this was once the fruit market. Look up at the glass roof, which protected the market traders from the rain and let in light – an important feature as they started work very early in the morning. In the old Apple Market you will find many craft stalls selling handmade toys, jewellery and clothing. Elsewhere in the central building there are all sorts of specialist shops, including a candle shop which, as well as selling an amazing variety of candles, shows you how they are made. There are many more fascinating shops in the streets off the main piazza, especially in James Street and Neal Street to the north. On the south side of the piazza is **Jubilee Market**, where you may find some interesting souvenirs. On Monday there are antiques stalls, but for the rest of the week there is a general and craft market.

Next door, in the old Flower Market, is **London's Transport Museum**, which tells the story of London's bus and Undergound services from the beginning of the nineteenth century to the present day and has many old vehicles on display. There are lots of videos and hands-on exhibits to play with, and at certain times actors help bring the displays to life. The oldest vehicles are horse-drawn buses from the 1830s, which carried limited numbers and were relatively expensive. The horse-drawn trams of the 1870s were more comfortable as they travelled on rails and the fares were more affordable as they could carry more passengers. Motor buses were developed in the twentieth century and there are several examples showing the changes from 1911 up to the present day. The history of the Underground is also explored. There is a train from the first line to be built, the Metropolitan Line of 1866. Steam locomotives were used until electric trains replaced them in the 1920s. A full-scale recreation of workmen digging a tunnel by candlelight conveys the cramped and difficult conditions in which they laboured. One of the most popular exhibits allows you to try your hand at driving a Tube train using a simulator with real controls.

LONDON'S TRANSPORT MUSEUM, Covent Garden Piazza, London WC2E 7BB.

Telephone: 020 7379 6344.

Website: www.ltmuseum.co.uk

Open: 10.00–18.00 (11.00–18.00 Friday).

continued opposite

Admission charge, but children aged under sixteen free.

Nearest Underground: Covent Garden, Leicester Square, Holborn.

Buses: 1, 4, 6, 9, 11, 13, 15, 23, 59, 68, 76, 77A, 91, 168, 171, 176, 188, 501, 521.

Nearby are a number of London's best-known West End theatres, so it is appropriate that in Russell Street is the **Theatre Museum**, describing the development of theatre and other forms of entertainment from Shakespeare's time to the present day. The displays include models, props and costumes from ballet, music hall, circus and pop music. You can see memorabilia of famous actors as well as a suit worn by one of the Beatles and Mick Jagger's jump-suit. There are regular special activities for children to take part in, such as puppet workshops and make-up demonstrations.

THEATRE MUSEUM, Russell Street, London WC2E 7PA.

Telephone: 020 7943 4700.

Website: www.theatremuseum.org

Open: Tuesday to Sunday 10.00–18.00.

Admission charge but free for those under sixteen or over sixty.

Nearest Underground: Covent Garden, Leicester Square, Holborn.

Buses: 1, 4, 6, 9, 11, 13, 15, 23, 59, 68, 76, 77A, 91, 168, 171, 176, 188, 501, 521.

Overlooking the piazza on the north side is the imposing **Royal Opera House**, home of the Royal Opera and the Royal Ballet. It reopened at the end of 1999 after extensive renovation which created a new entrance on to the piazza and turned the glass and iron Floral Hall into an attractive new foyer. The theatre has been criticised in the past for being inaccessible to many, but today some areas are open to the public and occasionally there are free exhibitions and musical events. There are also backstage tours which allow you to find out how this historic theatre operates.

ROYAL OPERA HOUSE, Bow Street, London WC2E 9DD.

Box office and information: 020 7304 4000.

Website: www.royaloperahouse.org

Backstage tours: Monday to Saturday 10.30, 12.30 and 14.30, unless there is an event during the day. (Charge.)

On some days it is possible to watch the ballet in class (for which a small fee is charged). Check with the box office.

Nearest Underground: Covent Garden, Leicester Square, Holborn.

Buses: 1, 4, 6, 9, 11, 13, 15, 23, 59, 68, 76, 77A, 91, 168, 171, 176, 188, 501, 521.

12
St Paul's Cathedral

St Paul's Cathedral is the masterpiece of Sir Christopher Wren, built to replace the church that had been destroyed in the Great Fire of London in 1666. It is the fifth church to occupy a site where according to legend a Roman temple to the goddess Diana used to stand. The first cathedral, a wooden church built in AD 604 by Bishop Mellitus, burnt down in 675. The second church was destroyed by Viking invaders, the third by fire in 1087, and the fourth, known as Old St Paul's, was the one destroyed in 1666, although it was already in a dilapidated state by then. Old St Paul's once had a 460 foot (140 metre) spire, the tallest ever built in England, which dominated the city skyline much as the present dome does today; it collapsed in 1561 after being struck by lightning and was never rebuilt. The church was regularly used for many non-religious purposes, with dentists and lawyers plying their trades within and all sorts of shops being set up on the tombs. In fact, so many people used it as a short-cut that the nave was called 'Paul's Walk'. To make matters worse, during the Civil War Cromwell's troops stabled their horses here and the woodwork was used for firewood.

Even before the Great Fire, Christopher Wren had been asked to prepare plans to

repair the old church, so he very quickly produced new plans for a completely new building. Over the next few years he produced several designs, all with a dome, but they were all rejected. The design that was finally accepted had both a dome and a spire but Wren was allowed to make changes to the design as work progressed and the idea of the spire was dropped. A classical building of this scale had never been built in England before and it posed all sorts of technical problems, particularly in the construction of the dome, so various adjustments had to be made and Wren, as a highly trained mathematician, loved solving problems.

The foundation stone was laid in 1675 and the church was consecrated in 1710, by which time Wren was an old man. He kept a very close eye on the building work throughout the thirty-five years of its construction, visiting it several times a week, when he would be carried up in a basket to inspect the work. While St Paul's was

St Paul's Cathedral seen from the Millennium Bridge.

Nelson's tomb in the crypt of St Paul's Cathedral.

going up, he managed to find the time to organise the building of fifty-one new City churches and the Royal Hospital in Chelsea. There were numerous complaints that the work was taking too long (at one stage Wren had his salary cut in half) but many problems slowed the project down, including severe winters and delays in the supply of stone, which had to come by sea from Portland in Dorset. When the last stone was ready to be placed on top of the lantern Wren was too weak to do it himself, so the task was carried out by his son.

The famous **dome** is a masterpiece of design and engineering. It is not quite what it seems and is actually a double dome. The outer dome is made of wood and is covered in lead. The lantern and cross on top weigh 700 tons and have to be supported by a brick cone hidden inside the outer dome. The dome you see from inside the Cathedral is very much lower, being inside the base of the cone.

Before going inside, take time to look at the impressive **west front**. Above the double row of columns is a triangular pediment with a carving of the Conversion of St Paul. Above that is a statue of St Paul carrying his emblem, a sword, which is used on the coat of arms of the City of London. On either side are two bell towers. In the right-hand tower is the 17 ton bell, Great Paul, which is tolled daily at 13.00; originally this was to remind apprentices it was time to return to work. Another smaller bell, Great Tom, chimes the hours and is also tolled on the death of royalty, the Archbishop of Canterbury or the Lord Mayor of the City of London. The statue in the forecourt is of Queen Anne, who was on the throne when the building was completed.

Once inside, stand at the back by the west door and look right down the **nave** towards the east end. You will notice how spacious and light the building is. Wren originally wanted all the windows to contain plain glass to allow as much light as possible to flood the church, and in the nave the windows still have no stained glass. Just inside the west door, on the floor, is a memorial to the St Paul's Firewatch. This was a team of people who spent the nights of the 1940 Blitz during the Second World War on the roof of the Cathedral looking out for firebombs and thus saving the church from destruction.

As you walk down the central aisle you will pass, on the left, an enormous monument which barely fits under the arch. This commemorates the Duke of Wellington, victor at the Battle of Waterloo in 1815, who is buried in the crypt. The Duke is shown at the top of the memorial on his favourite horse, Copenhagen. Walk on down the church until you are standing right under the crossing, where you can fully appreciate the size of the dome. Inside the dome are frescoes showing scenes from the life of St Paul painted by Sir James Thornhill. Once, while he was working

47

on the paintings, Thornhill stepped back to check his work and was close to falling off the scaffolding. A quick-thinking assistant splashed some paint on the wall and Thornhill stepped forward to tell him off, thus saving his life. The frescoes are best seen from the **Whispering Gallery**, which runs round the base of the dome. It is so called because if you whisper into the wall on one side you can be clearly heard on the other side. The entrance to the gallery is in the south aisle and there is a separate charge. You can also climb to the Golden Gallery at the top of the dome for superb views over London, but be warned – there are 627 steps. On the way up you can see the brick cone between the two domes.

Wren gathered around him some of the finest craftsmen of the day, the most famous being the woodcarver Grinling Gibbons, who carved the choir (or quire, as it is referred to in St Paul's) stalls and the organ case. The iron railings round the Whispering Gallery and the gates into the two choir aisles were made by Jean Tijou from France. The colourful mosaics around the dome and in the choir were added in the nineteenth century when the church was considered to be rather dull and dreary. At the east end is the figure of Christ in majesty and on the choir ceiling are animals, birds and fishes, including some wonderful spouting whales.

Go through the Tijou gates into the north choir aisle where, at the far end, you will see an even more splendid set of gates by Tijou. Opposite them is a sculpture called 'Mother and Child' by Henry Moore, who chose this spot because of the natural lighting. Behind the canopy over the high altar is the **American Memorial Chapel**, created as a tribute to the 28,000 Americans based in Britain who died in the Second World War. The wood carvings include many American birds and flowers as well as a space rocket hiding among foliage on the right-hand side. In the south choir aisle is a statue of the poet **John Donne**, who was Dean of St Paul's. He is shown in a shroud and posed for the sculpture wrapped in a sheet. This is the only statue to survive the fire in 1666 and you can still see the scorch marks around the base of the figure.

In the south transept is the entrance to the **crypt**, which is as big as the main church and is the largest in Europe. Turning right at the bottom of the steps, you come to the simple **tomb of Sir Christopher Wren**. Above it is the Latin inscription *Lector, si monumentum requiris, circumspice*, which means 'Reader, if you seek his monument, look around you'. Nearby is the massive marble tomb of the Duke of Wellington, resting on a base with four lions' heads at the corners. Lord Nelson is buried right under the dome in a black sarcophagus originally made for Henry VIII's Chancellor, Cardinal Wolsey. When Wolsey fell from favour the tomb was taken by Henry and lost for over two hundred years.

The way out is at the west end of the crypt, where you will also find toilets, a shop and a cafe.

ST PAUL'S CATHEDRAL, St Paul's Churchyard, London EC4M 8AD.

Telephone: 020 7246 8348.

Website: www.stpauls.co.uk

Open: Monday to Saturday 8.30–16.00 (last entry).

Admission charge.

Nearest Underground: St Paul's.

Buses: 4, 8, 11, 15, 17, 23, 25, 26, 56, 76, 100, 172, 242, 501, 521.

The Guildhall Art Gallery houses the City of London's art collection.

13
City walk

The City of London is the financial and economic centre of Britain and is full of banks, insurance companies and other financial institutions. Millions of pounds are made here every day as currencies, gold, tin, coffee and other commodities are bought and sold. London is such an important financial centre that there are now over five hundred foreign banks based in the City. About 300,000 people work in the City but only about 5000 live here. If you take the following walk on a weekday you will find a hive of activity but at weekends the streets are practically empty.

The City of London is often referred to as the Square Mile as this is roughly the area it covers (about 2.6 square km). It is still more or less within the third-century Roman walls and on the site of the medieval town. Despite all the rebuilding over the centuries, the street plan is still very much as it was then, with many narrow lanes and alleys running off the main roads. The street names have changed little and tell us much about the City's past.

The City, despite modernisation and new technology, still retains many of its old traditions, especially in the way its representatives are elected and the power of the trade guilds, or livery companies. It still has its own police force, whose helmets are different from those worn by the rest of London's policemen.

This walk is designed to take you past some of the major attractions in the City, both historic and modern. It is in two halves, each part lasting about an hour to an hour and a half, but if you miss out some of the attractions the whole walk could be done in about two hours.

ST PAUL'S TO BANK

Start at St Paul's Underground station and turn right into **Cheapside**. In the

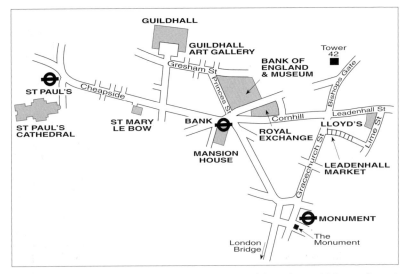

Middle Ages this was London's busy main street, with markets which overflowed into the side streets (*ceap* or *chepe* is the Old English word for market and also the source of the word 'shopping'). The names of the streets off to left and right, such as Milk Street, Bread Street and Wood Street, tell you what was sold there. Friday Street was where fish was sold on Friday, when meat was not supposed to be eaten. Cheapside was also a place for tournaments, processions and executions, which is why it is so wide.

On the left is Foster Lane with St Vedast's church, one of the many rebuilt by Sir Christopher Wren after the Great Fire of 1666. St Vedast (died 540) was a French bishop and 'Foster' is derived from his name, an example of how words can change with time. It is said that all true cockneys are born within the sound of the bells of **St Mary-le-Bow Church** on the right. This is probably because the curfew bell used to be rung from the tower, telling people to return within the walls of the city. Legend has it that the bells also persuaded Dick Whittington to return to London as they tolled out 'Turn again, turn again, thrice mayor of London'. Although much of the story, especially the part about his cat, is fictitious, he did indeed became mayor of London, but four times not three. The name of the church comes from the arches, or bows, on which it was built. The building was destroyed in 1666 and rebuilt by Wren, but it was badly damaged again in the Second World War and has been restored again. The steeple is very distinctive and has a weathervane in the shape of a dragon on the top. Royalty used to watch tournaments from a wooden balcony beside the old church and Wren included a balcony halfway up the new tower as a reminder. One of the more unusual places to have lunch around here is in the ancient crypt, which houses a vegetarian restaurant that is open Monday to Friday.

Alongside the church is a small garden with the statue of Captain John Smith, founder of Virginia. In 1608 his life was saved by the thirteen-year-old Indian princess, Pocahontas. She was later captured by settlers and married the tobacco planter John Rolfe. In 1616 she became the first American to visit England, where she met many important people, including King James I. The following year she fell ill aboard the ship taking her back to America and was brought ashore at Gravesend, where she died.

The next street on the left, King Street, leads to the **Guildhall**, the headquarters of the Corporation of London, the body which governs the City. It was built in the fifteenth century but was badly damaged in the Great Fire and again during the

Second World War. It is still used for local government meetings, state banquets and the annual election of the Lord Mayor. In front of the Guildhall is the church of St Lawrence Jewry, the Corporation church, which was restored after being bombed during the Blitz. The new building to the right is the Guildhall Art Gallery, where the extensive art collection of the City of London is housed. During its construction the remains of part of a Roman amphitheatre were found and have been preserved under the new building. In the courtyard there is a semicircular black marble line showing the ampitheatre's outline.

Unless it is being used for a function, it is possible to visit the **Great Hall** of the Guildhall. Around the walls hang the banners of the twelve most important guilds, or livery companies. These date from the Middle Ages, when they were formed to protect their members' interests and maintain standards of workmanship. Although they no longer serve these purposes, the guilds are still very powerful and wealthy institutions which carry out many charitable and educational works, and they still help elect the Lord Mayor. The windows carry the names of all the Lord Mayors with the dates they were in office. There are several monuments around the walls to outstanding national figures, including Lord Nelson, the Duke of Wellington and Winston Churchill. At one end of the hall is a minstrels' gallery with the figures of Gog and Magog, the legendary giants, which represent the ancient British and Trojan warriors whose war led to the creation of the town of New Troy on the site of present-day London. The originals were paraded through the streets at pageants and processions but were destroyed in the Blitz in 1940. A number of important people have been tried in the hall, including Archbishop Cranmer and Lady Jane Grey, the nine-day queen. In 1546 Anne Askew, a Protestant, was tried for heresy during the reign of Mary I and was tortured at the Tower, then burnt at Smithfield.

GUILDHALL, Gresham Street, London EC2P 2EJ.

Telephone: 020 7606 3030.

Open: May to September, daily 10.00–17.00; October to April, Monday to Saturday 10.00–17.00.

Admission free.

GUILDHALL ART GALLERY, Guildhall Yard, London EC2P 2EJ.

Telephone: 020 7332 3700.

Website: www.guildhall-art-gallery.org.uk

Open: Monday to Saturday 10.00–17.00; Sunday 12.00–16.00.

Admission charge, but free Saturday to Thursday after 15.30 and all day Friday.

Nearest Underground: St Paul's, Moorgate, Mansion House, Bank.

Buses: 4, 8, 25, 56, 100, 242, 501.

Outside the Guildhall turn left into Gresham Street, named after Thomas Gresham, an important Elizabethan merchant and financier who founded the Royal Exchange, which we will pass later in the walk. Off Gresham Street on the right is Old Jewry, a reminder that this was the main Jewish quarter of London until Edward I expelled the Jews in 1290. Turn right into Prince's Street, where the blank wall on the left is the outer wall of the **Bank of England**, the official government bank which advises the Chancellor of the Exchequer on economic policy, sets the interest rate, issues all England's banknotes and stores Britain's gold and currency reserves in its vaults. The bank was founded in 1694 to lend money to William III, who needed it to fight the French. It is often referred to as the 'Old Lady of Threadneedle Street', the street its main entrance is on. (The street used to be called Three Needles Street, the three needles being the coat of arms of the Needlemakers' Company, which used to have its hall here.) Round the corner in Bartholomew Lane is the **Bank of England Museum**, where you can find out more about the Bank's history and how it works.

BANK OF ENGLAND MUSEUM, Bartholomew Lane, London EC2R 8AH.

Telephone: 020 7601 5545.

Website: wwww.bankofengland.co.uk

Open: Monday to Friday 10.00–17.00; closed weekends and bank holidays, but open during the Lord Mayor's Show.

Admission free.

Nearest Underground: Bank.

Buses: 8, 11, 21, 23, 25, 26, 76, 133, 501.

With your back to the Bank, look over to the right and you will see the **Mansion House**, with its classical portico. This is the official residence of the Lord Mayor of the City of London during his year of office, and it is from here that the popular Lord Mayor's Show sets out every year in November (see Chapter 1). It was built in the eighteenth century; before that the Lord Mayor lived, worked and entertained in his own home. It is possible to visit the splendid interior, but you will need to apply in writing well in advance as there is a long waiting list.

Over to the left is the **Royal Exchange**. The first Exchange was built by Thomas Gresham and the building you see today is a replacement. Merchants originally carried out their trading in the open air. Gresham had seen such a building in Antwerp and decided to build one in London. It was opened by Elizabeth I, who was so impressed she insisted on calling it Royal. On the top of the building is the Gresham family crest, a golden grasshopper. At a time when many people were illiterate signs such as this helped them find where they were going. Indeed, some of today's companies still use these traditional symbols; if you take a short walk down Lombard Street you will see several more of these signs, including an anchor, a cat and fiddle, and a black horse, still the emblem of Lloyds TSB.

BANK TO LONDON BRIDGE

To begin the second half of this walk, go up Cornhill, the highest hill in the City, where in Saxon times corn was cultivated and sold. A little way up on the right is St Michael's Alley, where the Jamaica Wine House stands on the site of Pasqua Rosée's Head, the very first coffee house in London, which opened in 1652. Coffee houses were important places in the seventeenth and eighteenth centuries, where writers, actors and merchants met to hear the latest news and discuss the issues of the day. As we shall see, some very important institutions began life in coffee houses.

At Gracechurch Street look left up Bishopsgate to the tallest building in the City, Tower 42, once called the NatWest Tower. Cross into Leadenhall Street, where Richard (Dick) Whittington lived for a time and which is named after a medieval house that had a lead roof. On the right is **Lloyd's**, one of London's most distinctive modern buildings, designed by Richard Rogers and opened by the Queen in 1986. The most striking thing about the glass and steel structure is that many of the functional parts of the building, such as the lifts and pipes, are situated on the outside to make maintenance easier. Lloyd's started in 1688 as a shipping insurance company in Edward Lloyd's coffee house, where ships' captains and shipowners would meet and exchange shipping information.

Turn right down Lime Street and right again into Leadenhall Place. This brings you into **Leadenhall Market**, where there has been a market since the Middle Ages. The present building was erected in 1881 and the cast-iron structure has been

The Monument in Fish Street Lane commemorates the Great Fire of London.

attractively painted in bright colours. There are still a number of shops alongside restaurants and wine bars, which are at their busiest during weekday lunchtimes.

Turn left into Gracechurch Street, passing the headquarters of Barclay's Bank on the right. Straight ahead, in Fish Street Lane, is the **Monument**, a massive classical column topped by a gilded flaming urn and designed by Sir Christopher Wren to commemorate the Great Fire of London. It is 202 feet (61.6 metres) high and this is said to be the distance from its base to where the fire started in the royal bakery in Pudding Lane. (In this case 'pudding' has nothing to do with any dessert but refers to the offal from the butchers' shops in Eastcheap which was brought this way to be thrown into the river.) It is possible to climb to the top of the Monument for fine views over the City, but be warned – there are 311 steps and no lift. Everyone who climbs to the top is given a certificate.

> THE MONUMENT, Monument Street, London EC3 8AH.
>
> Telephone: 020 7626 2717.
>
> Open daily 10.00–17.40.
>
> Admission charge.
>
> Nearest Underground: Monument.
>
> Buses: 15, 17, 21, 25, 35, 40, 43, 47, 48, 133, 149, 501, 521.

You could end the walk here (Monument Underground station is nearby), but you may like to walk on to London Bridge for one of the best panoramic views in London, downstream to Tower Bridge and the Tower of London. The modern London Bridge is more or less on the site of the very first bridge built here by the Romans in the first century. In the twelfth century the famous stone bridge was erected; it was lined with houses and shops and had a chapel in the middle. Heads of traitors were stuck on poles above the gatehouse on the south side as a warning to the rest of the population. It was the only bridge over the river until 1750 and it was often so crowded that many people preferred to travel around London by boat, although navigating through the bridge was very dangerous and many people drowned. As the bridge slowed the flow, the Thames would freeze over in very cold winters and frost fairs were held on the ice. The medieval bridge was demolished to make way for a new bridge in 1831. In 1967, when the present bridge was started, an American company bought the nineteenth-century bridge and rebuilt it in the Arizona desert as a tourist attraction.

14
The Tower of London

In past centuries the threat of being 'sent to the Tower' caused terror. Its association with dank dungeons, horrible torture and executions is one of the main reasons for the Tower of London's continuing popularity among today's visitors, who have the consolation of knowing they will be able to leave at the end of their stay. Amongst the Tower's most popular exhibits are the priceless Crown Jewels, but the instruments of torture are also high on many people's list of things to see.

The Tower is guarded by the Yeoman Warders, popularly known as **Beefeaters**, who still wear traditional Tudor uniforms in dark blue and red for every day and red and gold for special ceremonial occasions. They offer regular tours and will entertain you with some of the more interesting and often blood-curdling stories associated with the Tower.

Since the eleventh century the Tower has been an impregnable fortress and one of several royal palaces in London, where the new king or queen used to spend the night before their coronation, processing through the streets to Westminster Abbey to be crowned. From its early days it was also used as a secure prison where state criminals, including royalty, could be locked away, though some of them managed to escape. More surprisingly, the Tower once housed the royal menagerie, which was later to form the basis of London Zoo – including gifts of leopards, lions and an elephant from foreign kings, and a polar bear presented by the King of Norway which was regularly to be seen bathing in the Thames.

Building was begun in 1078 by William I, the first Norman king, to protect the city from attack, but also to show his new subjects who was in charge. His building is the White Tower, a solid keep which is still at the heart of the complex and would once have seemed like a skyscraper compared to the surrounding buildings. The two outer rings of walls and towers as well as the moat were built by later kings to make it more secure from invaders, and the layout as we see it today was finished by 1300.

The way into the Tower today is through the **Middle** and **Byward Towers**, which were two of three towers protecting the entrance across the moat. The drawbridges have gone, but you can still see the portcullises which could be dropped to prevent attack. Look up at the arches and you will also see the 'murder holes' through which

A view of the Tower of London from across the river Thames.

missiles could be dropped on to attackers or water poured to put out a fire. The next tower is the **Bell Tower**, with a little wooden turret housing the curfew bell. Many important prisoners have been locked up here, including Thomas More and possibly Elizabeth I when she was a princess. Further on to the right is the infamous **Traitors' Gate**. This was originally built as the river entrance to the Tower, but in Henry VIII's time many state prisoners passed through the arch to await trial and back out again on their journey by boat to Westminster, where trials were usually held, guarded by a Yeoman Warder carrying an axe. If, on the return, the axe was pointing towards the prisoner, this meant he was guilty.

Opposite Traitors' Gate are two more towers. The large round one to the right is the **Wakefield Tower**, said to be where Henry VI was murdered and part of the royal apartments built in the thirteenth century. It can be visited as part of the restored Medieval Palace, in which some of the rooms have been recreated as they might have been originally and costumed actors help explain what life at court was like. The square tower above the gateway is the notorious **Bloody Tower**. Originally called the Garden Tower, as it was next to the Lieutenant's garden, its name was changed as it is thought the Princes in the Tower were murdered here in 1483. The princes, the twelve-year-old Edward V and his brother, Richard, were brought here for protection after the death of their father, Edward IV. They were never to leave the Tower and are presumed to have been smothered to death, some say on the orders of their uncle, the future Richard III. Bones found near the White Tower in 1674 were thought to be theirs and were reburied in Westminster Abbey. The great explorer Sir Walter Raleigh was imprisoned here for thirteen years and an extra floor was added to the tower to allow for his family to be accommodated. He spent much of his time writing and giving lessons to Henry, Prince of Wales, for whom he wrote his *History of the World* during his imprisonment. On the first floor you can see the massive windlass which was used to raise and lower the portcullis and which is still in full working order. To visit the Bloody Tower, go through the arch and turn left at the top of the steps.

Tower Green, the grassy area at the top of the steps, is overlooked by a number of houses, including the half-timbered Queen's House, which is home to the Governor. In a first-floor room of this house, Guy Fawkes, one of the Gunpowder Plot conspirators, was interrogated. Various prisoners have been detained here; the Earl of Nithsdale, who was imprisoned in 1715, carried out an unusual escape by dressing up in women's clothes smuggled in by his wife.

On the opposite side of Tower Green is the site of the **Execution Block**. Seven people were beheaded here, away from the gaze of the public. Among them were three queens of England, Lady Jane Grey and two of Henry VIII's wives, Ann Boleyn and Catherine Howard. They were all buried in unmarked graves in the **Chapel of St Peter ad Vincula**, which is behind the scaffold site. Only visitors on a Beefeater tour are able to visit the chapel.

By now you will no doubt have seen or heard some of the Tower's best-known inhabitants, the **ravens**. There have probably been ravens here as long as there has been a Tower as they are scavengers and would once have helped keep the area clean, no doubt enjoying the scraps from the kitchens. During the seventeenth century the Astronomer Royal worked in the Tower but found the ravens stopped him from doing his job properly. Charles II asked for the birds to be killed but was told of the tradition that if the ravens left the Tower the country would fall, so to this day a small number have been allowed to remain. Today there are six ravens, with one or two in reserve, and their wings are clipped so they cannot fly away. (One raven did apparently escape by climbing on to scaffolding on the White Tower and gliding out over the walls before being found on a nearby roundabout.) The ravens are well looked after by the Ravenmaster, who feeds them on raw meat and a dog biscuit soaked in blood every day. Every few weeks they are given a rabbit complete with its fur, which is good for their digestion. You can see the ravens' cages behind

The uniform of Yeoman Warders dates back to Tudor times.

the Wakefield Tower.

Close to the Chapel of St Peter is the spacious **Beauchamp Tower**, used by many of the wealthier aristocratic prisoners. Some of them left their mark, quite literally, as the first floor has many interesting inscriptions carved in the walls.

The **Crown Jewels** are kept in vaults under the Wellington Barracks to the north of the White Tower. There are often long queues to see them, but on the way in you can watch a film of the most important objects and how they are used. The jewels are the regalia used at Westminster Abbey for coronations. Most date from the time of Charles II, or later, as the majority of the earlier regalia was melted down during the Commonwealth. The oldest piece is the gold anointing spoon, which may have been used at the coronation of King John in 1199. The two crowns used for coronations are St Edward's Crown and the Imperial State Crown, which holds the Second Star of Africa, one of the largest diamonds in the world. The largest cut diamond, weighing 530 carats, can be found in the top of the sceptre. In the Queen Mother's Crown is the famous Koh-i-noor diamond from India. Its name means 'mountain of light', but it has had a violent history and is said to bring bad luck to any man who wears it, so since it arrived in England it has been worn only by women. Look for the small crown specially made for Queen Victoria, who found the Imperial State Crown too heavy.

The Norman **White Tower** is so called because it used to be covered in whitewash to protect it from the elements. The entrance is on the south side, up some wooden stairs, which is very much as it would have been when the tower was first built. The door was at first-floor level, and in case of attack the defenders could burn or destroy the stairs. On your way in, notice how thick the walls are – about 15 feet (4.8 metres) at this level. A spiral staircase takes you up to the Chapel Royal of St John, built to be used by the king and his family, now beautifully plain, although it would once have had painted decoration on the pillars and arches. In the next room you can see a massive fireplace and two garderobes, or toilets, built into the thick outer walls. The garderobe is a simple hole leading straight down into the moat, which would have been washed out twice a day by the Thames. This rather simple sanitary arrangement was important if the Tower was under attack, but it was also a security risk, as attackers could get into the building by this rather unpleasant route.

Next door are displays of arms and armour from the Tudor and Stuart periods. The most impressive pieces were made for Henry VIII, including a suit made for tournaments with many attachments for different types of combat. By the time the armour was made Henry was obese, old and sickly, but he had been very athletic as a young man. You may be surprised by the prominent codpiece, but this was a standard part of male dress at the time. Nearby is a 20 foot (6 metre) wooden lance used in tournaments – it is hollow to make it lighter, but it must still have been very

The ravens are amongst the most famous inhabitants of the Tower.

heavy. There are also some highly decorative suits of armour made for Charles I and his brother, Prince Henry. One of the most unusual objects on display is a suit of Japanese armour sent to James I in 1613.

On the next floor are displays of weapons and barrels of gunpowder, as this was once the Ordnance, where such things were stored. Stairs take you down to the Small Armoury, which is a recreation of the decorative way weapons would have been displayed in the seventeenth and eighteenth centuries. The Spanish Armoury contains an execution block and executioner's sword. The massive axe dates from the sixteenth century. The block was used for the execution of Lord Lovat, the last person to be beheaded on Tower Hill, in 1747. The way out is through the basement, where you can see the deep well which supplied the castle with fresh water.

The Tower is locked up every night at 22.00 in an ancient ceremony called the **Ceremony of the Keys**. It is possible to attend this short but poignant piece of the Tower's pageantry (see Chapter 1).

TOWER OF LONDON, Tower Hill, London EC3N 4AB.

Telephone: 020 7709 0765.

Website: www.hrp.org.uk

Open: March to October, Monday to Saturday 9.00–17.00, Sunday 10.00–17.00; November to February, Tuesday to Saturday 9.00–16.00, Sunday to Monday 10.00–16.00.

Admission charge.

Nearest Underground: Tower Hill.

Buses: 15, 25, 42, 78, 100.

15
Tower Bridge

Tower Bridge is one of London's best-known and most easily recognised landmarks. Built in the late nineteenth century, it can open up to allow large ships to pass in and out of the Pool of London. Underneath its ancient-looking Gothic stonework the marvels of late-Victorian engineering can be seen and admired because the bridge is open as a museum.

When Tower Bridge was first proposed, the area just downstream of London Bridge was still a very busy port, so any new bridge had to allow ships to pass through it. Many complicated plans were put forward by the most eminent architects and engineers of the time, and the design by Horace Jones was chosen. Because of the complex technology and the fact that the river had to be kept clear during construction, the bridge took eight years to build, and its erection was followed with great interest by curious Londoners. The official opening by the Prince of Wales on 30th June 1894 was a day of great pomp and ceremony, with grandstands put up along the river bank and hundreds of boats of all sizes, decked with flags and bunting, crowding the river itself. The royal party drove along the road in open carriages, then the Prince pushed a button to open the roadway to allow the first ships through.

The bridge was originally operated by hydraulic engines and the 1000 ton bascules (the two halves of the road which open) took about six minutes to open fully. Today they use electric power and take only ninety seconds, but it is still an impressive sight when the road opens up and the two halves rise slowly to their full height. When the bridge was new it opened as many as twenty times a day, but now that the river is less busy it opens only a few times a week. In 1912 Frank McLean became the first person to fly a plane through the bridge, and in 1952 a bus driver found the bridge opening up underneath him and had to 'jump' his bus across the gap.

The high-level walkways between the towers were built to allow people to cross the river when the bridge opened, but so few used them that they were closed in 1910. Today they are open to the public again and the views from them are one of the main reasons for visiting the Tower Bridge Experience. The entrance is at the base of the north tower, where you take one of the lifts up to the exhibition, which tells the story of the bridge and its construction. You meet the chatty animatronic figure of Harry the painter and the ghost of Horace Jones, who explains his designs. The walkways give you panoramic views across London, westwards over the City and as far as the Houses of Parliament, and eastwards towards Docklands, including Canary Wharf with its flashing beacon. When you leave by the south tower, you can continue to the south side of the bridge, visiting the old engine rooms to see some of the original machinery used to operate the bridge.

TOWER BRIDGE EXPERIENCE, Tower Bridge, London SE1 2UP.

Telephone: 020 7940 3985. Schools programme: 020 7407 9191.

To find out when the bridge opens telephone 020 7940 3984.

Website: www.towerbridge.org.uk

Open: April to October 10.00–18.30; November to March 9.30–18.00.

continued opposite

Tower Bridge is over a hundred years old and now houses an exhibition about its construction and history.

Admission charge.
Nearest Underground: Tower Hill, London Bridge, Tower Gateway (DLR).
Buses: 15, 25, 42, 78, 100.

On the north bank of the Thames to the east of Tower Bridge are the **St Katharine Docks**, built in the 1820s by the great engineer Thomas Telford. When London's port began to close down and move downstream, these docks were the first to be redeveloped in the 1970s. Many of the old warehouses were refurbished for commercial use and a yacht marina was created. It is now a pleasant place to wander, and there are a number of shops and eating places. The marina is always full of interesting boats, including a number of Thames barges, with their distinctive red-brown sails.

16
The Museum of London

The Museum of London is the place to go to find out how London grew and developed, starting with prehistoric man and coming right up to the present day. It is the largest city history museum in the world, with vast collections of costume, furniture, paintings, photographs and everyday household objects, all of which help to tell the story of London in an exciting way. The museum is located in the corner of the Barbican development to the north of St Paul's Cathedral. Take care to follow the signs because the building can be a little difficult to find as it is not at street level. The museum regularly puts on special exhibitions and fascinating discoveries are frequently made, so new objects are often being added to the permanent displays. There are special events and activities for children, especially at weekends and during the holidays. A museum activity book for children called *London Alive!* is on sale in the shop.

From 2001 there will be some disruption as the whole museum undergoes a major redevelopment programme. Some galleries will inevitably have to close, but there will always be plenty to see.

The **Roman gallery** is rich in all sorts of objects excavated from under the streets of the city. *Londinium* was set up as a trading city, and there are examples of different objects from all over the Roman empire: pottery from France, glass from Germany and jewellery from Belgium. There is a display about Roman games, including dice, whistles and what looks like a wooden yo-yo. A number of shops and houses have been recreated to give you an idea of how the Romans lived: in the

glass and leather workshops and the builder's yard real tools of the period are used. There are also four rooms, including a kitchen and an elegant dining room complete with painted walls and a mosaic floor which would have covered an under-floor heating system.

One of the most exciting of recent finds was a stone sarcophagus discovered in Spitalfields in 1999. Inside was a lead coffin containing the well-preserved remains of a young Roman woman, complete with jet ornaments and glass bottles. A reconstruction of her head, using the skull as a guide, was made for a television programme about the discovery and is on show.

In the medieval displays look out for a rare child's cradle, with birds at each end to watch over the sleeping baby. There is also a good collection of leather shoes from

The skeleton and coffin of the Spitalfields Roman woman, with a model of how she looked when alive.

the thirteenth and fourteenth centuries, including one with a very long pointed toe. Pilgrimages were very popular in the Middle Ages and there are several interesting 'pilgrim badges', which were bought as souvenirs of a visit to one of the major shrines, especially the shrine of Thomas Becket, London's own saint, at Canterbury.

The Tudor galleries are overseen by a portrait of Henry VIII, with an example of armour made at his armouries at Greenwich. Look out for the **Cheapside Hoard**, a stunning display of jewellery and watches found in Cheapside in 1912. They probably come from stock hidden by a goldsmith for safe keeping during the Civil War. There is a recreation of a seventeenth-century room, complete with furniture and an early baby-walker.

In 1665 the **Great Plague** killed 25 per cent of the population of London. On display is a Plague bell, which was rung to warn people the carts were coming to carry away the dead. Also here is one of the Bills of Mortality, listing the deaths week by week. In the following year the Great Fire destroyed four-fifths of London. The **Great Fire Experience** is a dramatic telling of the story using a model of the city, with special effects showing the spread of the fire, accompanied by readings from Samuel Pepys's diaries.

From the Georgian period, the **Lord Mayor's Coach** is sumptuously painted in gold and red and richly decorated. It is the actual coach used in the Lord Mayor's Show every November. It was built in 1757 and has been in use ever since. The eighteenth-century displays are full of the beautiful clothes, musical instruments and jewellery of the well-to-do, including a dolls' house in the form of an elegant mansion. The darker side of life is illustrated by the grim, graffiti-covered walls of a cell from Wellclose Square Prison and a door from the notorious Newgate Prison.

Look out for the recreation of a school classroom from 1870, when state-run education first began. The furniture is original, with the blackboard and easel and elevated teacher's desk. There are lots of shops from the late nineteenth and early twentieth centuries including a grocer's shop complete with all its original fittings. Look out for the model butcher's shop, which was a popular toy of the period.

There are interesting displays on the Suffragette Movement, which campaigned for votes for women before the First World War. There are banners and posters, as well as the chains Suffragettes used to tie themselves to the railings of 10 Downing Street in 1908. Also on display is an early motorised London taxi from 1908, with its white wheels, polished brass and driver's cab open to the elements. There is also a horse-drawn hansom cab of the sort you see in Sherlock Holmes films. One of the largest and most impressive exhibits in the museum is a highly decorated lift from Selfridges. When it was installed in the store in 1928 it was operated by women in trousers, something not considered proper at the time. There is also a counter from an early Woolworth's store, with a sign declaring 'Nothing in these stores over 6d'.

MUSEUM OF LONDON, 150 London Wall, London EC2Y 5HN.

Telephone: 020 7600 3699. Fax: 020 7600 1058.

Website: www.museumoflondon.org.uk

Open: Monday to Saturday 10.00–17.50; Sunday 12.00–17.50 (last admission 17.30).

Admission charge, but ticket valid for one year. Children under 16 free, as well as visitors arriving after 16.30.

Nearest Underground: St Paul's, Barbican, Moorgate.

Buses: 4, 8, 25, 56, 100, 172, 242, 501, 521.

Pre-booked school visits in term-time are free. Telephone bookings can be made on 020 7814 5777. Various activity sheets and packs are available.

17
The British Library

The British Library is the country's national library and, by law, has to receive a copy of every new book published in Britain. For many years it was housed in the British Museum but in 1997 it moved into a purpose-built building in the Euston Road, which took more than twenty years to build, at a cost of over £500 million. It is not like a public lending library; its eleven reading rooms are used by students and researchers and you need to get a ticket to use it. It also has three fascinating exhibition galleries open to the general public. The huge red-brick building is entered via a large open piazza dominated by a colossal statue of Isaac Newton by Edward Paolozzi. Beneath the piazza are basements which stretch under the entire building and contain twelve million books. The interior of the building is surprisingly light and spacious. The three exhibition galleries are to the left, past a statue of Shakespeare.

The **John Ritblat Gallery** contains the main treasures of the library. In a very varied collection are many important historical documents, of which the most significant are two of the remaining copies of **Magna Carta**, on which the barons forced King John to put his seal at Runnymede in 1215. Also here is the prayer-book that Lady Jane Grey carried to her execution in 1554 and the diary written by Captain Scott on his fateful journey to the South Pole in 1912. Among the literary items are the first collected edition of Shakespeare's plays (the *First Folio* of 1623), and the original manuscript of Lewis Carroll's *Alice's Adventures Under Ground* (as *Alice in Wonderland* was first called), complete with the author's own drawings. There are many musical manuscripts on display, including Handel's *Messiah*, Elgar's *Enigma Variations* and several Beatles lyrics. Around the walls are earphones allowing you to hear extracts of music and speech related to the displays.

The gallery also contains many beautiful illuminated manuscripts, such as the seventh-century *Lindisfarne Gospels*, and sacred texts from different religions around the world. Look out for the fourteenth-century *Luttrell Psalter*, decorated with detailed scenes of everyday life. There is also a display of early maps, including a thirteenth-century map of Britain, and a world map of 1490, two years before Columbus discovered America.

The Workshop of Words, Sounds and Images is not so much an exhibition as an interactive, hands-on display, showing how books have been made throughout the ages. There are materials to handle, a desktop publishing computer to use and videos showing how paper is made and how medieval manuscripts were created. On Saturdays there are free demonstrations of calligraphy, printing and bookbinding. The Pearson Gallery houses exhibitions on a variety of related subjects which change regularly.

Back in the foyer, go up the stairs past the statue of Shakespeare and you will find an impressive glass tower filled with books from the King's Library, the collection of George III. They are not displayed like this simply for show, as a system of lifts and stairs means all the books can be taken out by staff if needed. Along the walls to the left are the philatelic collections, with about 80,000 early stamps from all over the world.

BRITISH LIBRARY, 96 Euston Road, London NW1 2DB.
Telephone: 020 7412 7332. Education Department: 020 7412 7797. Fax: 020 7412 7340.
Website: www.bl.uk
Open: Monday and Wednesday to Friday 9.30–18.00; Tuesday 9.30–20.00; Saturday 9.30–17.00; Sunday and bank holidays 11.00–17.00.
Admission free.
Nearest Underground: King's Cross St Pancras.
Buses: 10, 30, 73, 91.

18
British Museum

The British Museum houses one of the world's greatest collections of antiquities and cultural treasures from all round the world, including Greek sculpture, Roman mosaics, Egyptian mummies, Mexican carvings, Chinese bronzes and North American Indian head-dresses. It is also one of London's busiest museums, so be prepared for crowds.

The museum was founded in 1753 when the government bought the collections of Sir Hans Sloane. Sloane was a doctor, botanist and antiquarian who during his long life had built up a huge collection of antiques, plant specimens and books. (While in Jamaica he had seen the locals drinking a bitter drink made from cacao seeds; he added milk and sugar to create milk chocolate.) Other important collections were added and the museum opened in 1759 in a house in Bloomsbury, but with very limited access. Today's museum was built in the nineteenth century and is visited by about six million people every year. The British Library used to occupy part of the building, including the famous round Reading Room, but in 1997 it moved to a modern building in the Euston Road (see Chapter 17). The space around the Reading Room has been cleared to create the Queen Elizabeth II Great Court, with a spectacular new glass and steel roof. This is now the heart of the museum and it stays open later than the museum galleries every evening. In the Reading Room you can access the Compass database to find out more about the museum's collections. The information desks can tell you about any special exhibitions that are on and sell tickets for guided tours of the museum. They also sell an inexpensive guide to help you find your way around the galleries, though you will find the museum well signposted.

The Egyptian sculpture gallery contains a vast array of statues of pharaohs and priests, and gods with bird or animal heads, as well as smaller items of jewellery and a beautiful black cat with earrings. The most important object in the gallery is a rather plain dark stone called the **Rosetta Stone**. If you look closely you will see that it has an inscription in three different scripts: at the top are hieroglyphics; next is another Egyptian writing called Demotic; and at the bottom is Greek. Because the Greek could be read, the stone allowed experts to decipher hieroglyphs for the first time and meant they could read inscriptions of the sort you can see all around you in the gallery and understand ancient Egyptian life and customs.

In the upstairs Egyptian galleries you will find the most popular objects in the museum, a wonderful collection of **Egyptian mummies** and mummy cases, many of them intricately and colourfully decorated. You can see the way bodies were carefully wrapped in bandages, often creating beautiful geometric patterns. Also here are many of the objects left in the tombs for the deceased to use in the afterlife. Look out for the mummified animals, including cats and birds. The oldest mummy is that of a man who died around 3500 BC; it was well preserved by the hot sands of the desert. He is known as Ginger because of the colour of his hair.

On the ground floor are several galleries showing wonderfully lifelike Assyrian wall carvings. Nearby are two massive winged human-headed bulls which would once have guarded the entrance to an Assyrian palace. They both have five legs, so they could be seen to be stationary from the front, but moving from the side. The walls of the galleries are covered with lively scenes of military triumphs which would once have lined the walls of the palaces. One sequence shows King Ashurbanipal taking part in a lion hunt; the lions are realistically portrayed in various stages of dying, with arrows piercing their bodies and blood pouring from their mouths.

The Great Court of the British Museum.

The Duveen Gallery houses what are considered to be some of the greatest sculpture in the world, the **Elgin Marbles**. They were created in the fifth century BC to adorn the Parthenon in Athens but were acquired by Lord Elgin in 1801–3 and later sold to the British Museum. At each end of the room are statues which were once high up on each end of the temple and tell of moments in the life of Athena, the goddess of Athens. Smaller sculptures, called metopes, show lively scenes of men fighting with centaurs, half-man and half-horse. Around the walls is a relief depicting a religious procession, with soldiers on horseback and in chariots, and in the middle of one side a row of gods watching the celebrations. Special displays, including a video, show how the sculptures would have looked on the Parthenon, painted in bright colours.

One of the most beautiful objects in the museum is the **Portland Vase**, made in Rome in about 25 BC of two different coloured glasses, the blue glass covered in a white layer which has been cut away in a design showing scenes from Roman mythology. In 1845 a young student smashed it into nearly two hundred pieces but it has been skilfully glued back together again.

The Roman Britain gallery contains a wide-ranging display of mosaics, jewellery, statues and coins. Look out for the wooden writing tablets from Hadrian's Wall, which reveal what life was like in the Roman army. One of the finest objects in the gallery is the silver **Mildenhall Great Dish**, which shows a scene of figures dancing round the bearded head of a sea-god. In the Later Bronze Age gallery is the well-preserved body of **Lindow Man**, found in a peat bog in Cheshire in 1984 and sometimes referred to as 'Pete Marsh'. At first it was thought he was the victim of a recent murder, but we now know he died around 300 BC, probably as a sacrificial victim, as he had been hit over the head, strangled and his throat had been cut.

One of the most important archaeological finds in Britain during the twentieth century was the **Sutton Hoo** ship burial, discovered in Suffolk in 1939. It was probably the grave of an important East Anglian king, and he was surrounded by many of his personal possessions, including a richly decorated helmet, silver bowls and some beautiful gold jewellery inlaid with garnets and glass.

Two galleries are devoted to the art and culture of the Americas. The **North America Gallery** has changing displays of clothing, textiles and jewellery giving an idea of the lives of the indigenous tribes before and after the arrival of the Europeans. The **Mexican Gallery** has a fine collection of carvings, pottery and jewellery from the country's many different cultures, including a stunning double-headed serpent covered in turquoise mosaic.

BRITISH MUSEUM, Great Russell Street, London WC1B 3DG.

Telephone: 020 7323 8000.

Website: www.thebritishmuseum.ac.uk

Open: Museum: Saturday to Wednesday 10.00–17.30; Thursday to Friday 10.00–20.30. Great Court: Monday 9.00–18.00; Tuesday to Wednesday 9.00–21.00; Thursday to Saturday 9.00–23.00; Sunday 9.00–21.00.

Admission free.

Nearest Underground: Tottenham Court Road, Holborn, Russell Square.

Buses: 1, 7, 8, 10, 19, 24, 25, 29, 38, 55, 73, 98, 134, 242.

19
Madame Tussaud's and Regent's Park

There is more than enough to keep you busy in and around Regent's Park, as two of London's most popular attractions are to be found near here and there is plenty to do in the park itself.

If you arrive via Baker Street Underground you will find outside the Marylebone Road exit a larger-than-life statue of Sherlock Holmes, Arthur Conan Doyle's famous fictional detective, who had rooms round the corner at 221B Baker Street. Although this address never really existed, a **Sherlock Holmes Museum** has been created in a Victorian house at 239 Baker Street, with a Victorian policeman outside

to greet you. The house has been decorated and furnished according to the descriptions in the books and is full of authentic touches, such as a meerschaum pipe and deerstalker hat lying on a table, a violin propped up against the wall and scientific equipment waiting to be used for an experiment. On the top two floors there are life-size figures of various characters from the stories. Sherlock Holmes is such a famous detective that people still write to him, and there are recent letters on display from people asking for his help. Children familiar with the stories from books or on television will no doubt enjoy a visit to the museum.

The statue of Sherlock Holmes outside Baker Street Underground station.

SHERLOCK HOLMES MUSEUM, 221B Baker Street, London NW1 6XE.
Telephone: 020 7935 8866.
Website: www.sherlock-holmes.co.uk
Open: daily 9.30–18.00.
Admission charge.
Nearest Underground: Baker Street.
Buses: 2, 13, 18, 27, 30, 74, 82, 113, 139, 189, 274.

The actress Barbara Windsor at the unveiling of her likeness in Madame Tussaud's.

A short way along Marylebone Road is **Madame Tussaud's**, the famous wax museum. It is easy to spot because of the green dome of the Planetarium, which is in the same building. Madame Tussaud's is one of London's most popular attractions and you should expect a long queue during the summer and the school holidays. You can jump the queue if you have a timed admission ticket, booked in advance (telephone: 0870 400 3000).

Marie Grosholtz worked in Paris in the 1770s making wax models for Dr Curtius's wax exhibition. During the French Revolution she was imprisoned in the Bastille, but she was freed on the condition that she made death masks of the victims

of the guillotine. When Curtius died she took over the business and married an engineer called François Tussaud. In 1802 she brought her exhibition to England and toured for thirty-three years before finding a more permanent site for it in London. Some of her original work still survives and her self-portrait, the last model she made before her death at the age of eighty-nine, is one of the first things you see.

Your visit starts with the Garden Party, where you mingle with the current stars of screen, stage or sport. This section is regularly updated as fashions change.

The Hollywood Legends and Superstars area depicts some of the most famous actors and musicians, such as Charlie Chaplin, Marilyn Monroe, Michael Caine and Michael Jackson. The Grand Hall is the heart of the collection, with royalty, politicians, artists and religious leaders from all round the world. Here are many English kings and queens, including Henry VIII and his six wives and the present

The waxwork figure of Henry VIII at Madame Tussaud's.

royal family. Several American presidents are on display, including Madame Tussaud's own figure of George Washington. The family of the French king Louis XVI are also Madame Tussaud's originals. Here too are the Archbishop of Canterbury, the Pope, Nelson Mandela and Diana, Princess of Wales. The costumes are all carefully researched, using all the right materials for the period, and today's figures usually wear clothes donated by the sitter.

Down in the basement is the ever-popular Chamber of Horrors, where various methods of torture are shown alongside figures of famous murderers such as Dr Crippen and the 'brides in the bath' murderer, George Smith. You can also see the original door of the condemned cell of Newgate Prison and death masks of victims of the guillotine made from casts by Madame Tussaud during the French Revolution, including those of Louis XVI and Marie Antoinette. The visit ends with a ride in a miniature taxi in which you are taken through the Spirit of London, a quick history of London peopled with famous personalities, such as Shakespeare writing one of his plays and Wren directing the building of St Paul's Cathedral.

MADAME TUSSAUD'S, Marylebone Road, London NW1 5LR.

Telephone: 0870 400 3000.

Website: www.madame-tussauds.com

Open: Monday to Friday 10.00–17.30; Saturday, Sunday and bank holidays 9.30–17.30. Earlier opening during summer and school holidays.

Admission charge.

Nearest Underground: Baker Street.

Buses: 2, 13, 18, 27, 30, 74, 82, 113, 139, 189, 274.

The **London Planetarium** is in the same complex as Madame Tussaud's and takes you on an amazing journey into space under its giant dome. On the way in there are scale models and interactive displays explaining some of the mysteries of the cosmos and space exploration. The show itself uses the most advanced technology to take you on a futuristic high-speed journey through our galaxy and beyond, exploring a giant black hole and seeing the creation of new stars and planet systems.

LONDON PLANETARIUM, Marylebone Road, London NW1 5LR.

Telephone: 0870 400 3000.

Website: www.london-planetarium.com

Open: shows every 30 minutes from 12.30 (10.00 weekends and school holidays); last show 17.00.

Admission charge (combined ticket with Madame Tussaud's available).

Nearest Underground: Baker Street.

Buses: 2, 13, 18, 27, 30, 74, 82, 113, 139, 189, 274.

To the north of Marylebone Road is **Regent's Park**, one of the largest of the Royal Parks. It was laid out in the early nineteenth century for the Prince Regent (the future George IV) by John Nash. Originally there were to be a summer palace and many villas in the park, but only a few were built, including the elegant cream-coloured terraces which you can occasionally glimpse through the trees. There are many things to do in the park: lots of grass for ball games or picnics, a boating lake, and summer concerts from the bandstand overlooking the lake. An unusual feature to the west is the minaret of the Central London Mosque. In the heart of the park are the lovely **Queen Mary's Gardens**, named after the wife of George V, who was a keen gardener. They include a wonderful rose garden with almost four hundred different varieties. Nearby is the **Open Air Theatre**, which puts on Shakespeare plays and the occasional musical between May and September. On a balmy summer's evening it can be a delightful experience to be in the audience of *A Midsummer Night's Dream*. However, it is a good idea to wrap up warm, as even in the hottest summer the nights can get chilly.

OPEN AIR THEATRE, Regent's Park, London NW1.

Telephone: 020 7486 2431.

Website: www.open-air-theatre.org.uk

Nearest Underground: Regent's Park.

Buses: 2, 13, 18, 27, 30, 74, 82, 113, 139, 189, 274.

In the north-east corner of the park is the **London Zoo**, one of London's best attractions for families, allowing children to get close to a huge variety of wildlife from around the world. The zoo opened here in 1828, and among its first inhabitants were the animals once displayed at the Tower. Today there are over 12,000 animals, from giraffes to scorpions, lions to tarantulas. There are many examples of endangered species, as the zoo's main purposes today are conservation and education, and it carries out breeding programmes to help reintroduce some of the rarest animals into the wild. To help plan your visit, check the events leaflet for the numerous interesting things going on at different times throughout the day, including animal rides, seeing the penguins being fed or watching the elephants having a bath. The children can even have their faces painted as an animal – tigers are very popular – and there is a special children's zoo where they can get close to a range of domesticated animals such as sheep, pigs and ducks.

There is a recommended route around the zoo, painted on the ground in green. This takes you past all the main exhibits, but there are maps at regular intervals if you want to locate anything in particular. The big cats are particularly popular, including lions, leopards and the extremely rare, and rather secretive, Sumatran tiger. It is worth exploring the Moonlight World, home to animals which come out at night. Once you get used to the dark you can make out lemurs, sloths and bug-eyed bushbabies slowly moving around their cages. The reptile house, with its slithering rattlesnakes, pythons and alligators, always holds a strong fascination. The aquarium may not be as impressive as more modern versions elsewhere, but there are lots of fish of all shapes and sizes, from sharks and piranhas to the tiny but brightly coloured clownfish.

A new attraction is the Web of Life exhibition, which explains the great diversity of living creatures and the habitats they live in. It also highlights the impact humans are having on the ecology of the planet and the conservation work being carried out by the zoo. There is a wealth of live exhibits, including lots of insects such as praying mantises, scorpions, locusts and spiders. One ingenious exhibit allows you to watch naked mole rats moving around their complex of underground tunnels.

The closest Underground station to the Zoo is Camden Town (about fifteen minutes away), but bear in mind that at weekends you cannot leave by this station until after 17.30 because of the vast crowds going to Camden Market. If you plan to leave early you should therefore catch one of the buses.

LONDON ZOO, Regent's Park, London NW1 4RY.

Telephone: 020 7722 3333. Fax: 020 7586 6177.

Website: www.zsl.org

continued overleaf

The penguins at London Zoo.

Open: daily, winter 10.00–16.00, summer 10.00–17.30.
Admission charge.
Nearest Underground: Camden Town.
Buses: 274 from Oxford Circus, Baker Street or Camden Town.

The **Regent's Canal** runs through the middle of the zoo. This connects the river Thames with the rest of the canal system and was built to boost trade, but unfortunately it came too late and the business was taken away by the new-fangled railways. It is now used mostly by companies offering leisure trips in traditional narrowboats. One such company is the London Waterbus Company (telephone: 020 7482 2550), which runs an hourly service to the Zoo from Little Venice or Camden Town. From April to September the boats run daily, but from October to March they run at weekends only.

The statue of Guy the gorilla at London Zoo.

20
South Kensington museums

Three of London's most popular museums can be found close together in South Kensington, a short walk from Hyde Park and less than five minutes from South Kensington Underground station. They are the Natural History Museum, the Science Museum and the Victoria and Albert Museum, the first two being among the most child-friendly in London. It is worth walking through the tunnel which goes straight from the station to the museums to avoid the busy Cromwell Road.

The **Natural History Museum** tells the fascinating and complex story of the Earth from its creation millions of years ago to the present day and even takes a tentative look into the future. The museum has two main parts: the Life Galleries, covering the great diversity of lifeforms which have lived on the planet, and the Earth Galleries, dealing with the planet itself, including what goes on under the surface. The building, which dates from 1881, was very modern for its time, being constructed with iron and steel; it is covered in delightful carvings of animals, fish and plants, both inside and out. Most of the exhibitions are thoroughly modern, with touch screens, videos and interactive displays. You will need to be selective as there is too much to see in one visit.

The Tyrannosaurus rex model in the Natural History Museum stands 4 metres high and is nearly 7 metres long.

In the **Life Galleries** the main hall sets the scene with an introduction to the various displays in the museum. It is dominated by a replica of an enormous skeleton of a Diplodocus dinosaur, 84 feet (25 metres) long. The displays round the edges are highlights from the collections: a fossilised tree, insects trapped in amber, the skeleton of a dodo (extinct since 1693), and a coelacanth – a fish thought to have become extinct 70 million years ago until rediscovered in 1938.

The museum's most popular display is on **dinosaurs**. A raised walkway allows you to get close to several prehistoric beasts, from the massive Triceratops to the relatively tiny Dromaeosaurus. At the end of the gallery is a realistic tableau showing a huge animatronic Tyrannosaurus rex eating a recently killed Tenontosaurus. The exhibition explores the world of the dinosaurs, how they lived and what they ate – you may be surprised to find that most of them were vegetarian. A number of theories are offered for their sudden demise 65 million years ago. The remains of new dinosaurs are still being discovered and there is a display about one nicknamed 'Claws' found in a claypit in Surrey in 1983.

The displays of mammals are rather more traditional, with lots of stuffed animals in display cases. A huge variety of mammals is shown, from the tiny pigmy shrew to the hippopotamus. In one gallery a full-scale model of a **blue whale** dwarfs all the other mammals around it, even the elephant and giraffe. Other displays tell the story of sea mammals, including such extraordinary creatures as the dugongs and manatees, and an interactive exhibit allows you to match your intelligence with that of a dolphin.

The **Human Biology** section explores how the human body and mind work. Starting with cells, the basis of all life, it takes you through reproduction, birth and growing up, using remarkable videos of a growing foetus and all sorts of games and models explaining the workings of muscles, bones and the brain. A popular section illustrates with clever hands-on displays just how easily our eyes can play tricks on us.

Another popular gallery is **Creepy Crawlies**, where you can find out all about arthropods such as spiders, crabs, millipedes and termites. Among all the models and interactive displays is a real colony of leafcutter ants, busy cutting and collecting leaves to take back to the cut-away nest. The **Ecology** exhibition on the environment investigates how everything interconnects and the impact of humans on the world. You can learn about the food chain, how plants turn energy into food, and how a dead rabbit is recycled.

A walk through the bird gallery takes you to the **Earth Galleries**, housed in what used to be the Geological Museum – there is still a separate entrance, so you could start your visit here. At the start an escalator takes you up through the centre of a giant globe to the second floor. Here, in **The Power Within** gallery, vivid and often noisy, displays reveal how volcanoes happen, the different types of lava, and some of the benefits of volcanic activity such as fertile soil and good building stone. In a recreation of a Japanese supermarket you can experience aspects of the 1995 Kobe earthquake, with the floor moving violently in all directions. The **Restless Surface** section deals with the way the Earth's surface has been shaped by the forces of nature – wind, water, heat and ice – and there are lots of hands-on exhibits to try. Look out for the bolt of lightning frozen in sand. In **From the Beginning** you look at the creation of the solar system 4560 million years ago, and in particular at the creation of the Earth and how life developed. There are lots of fossils, including the head of a terrifyingly large prehistoric crocodile. **Earth's Treasury** has a vast collection of minerals and rocks, including many sparkling gemstones, showing how they were created and how we use them.

In the basement of the main building is the hands-on **Investigate Centre** for children aged seven to eleven. During term-time it is available for pre-booked school groups, but it is open to families at weekends and during school holidays.

In the grounds of the museum is a wildlife garden, with trees and wild flowers from different British habitats. Tours of the garden take place twice a day in spring and summer, depending on the weather, and can be booked at the admissions desk. School groups can book a tour as part of a museum visit.

A new attraction due to open in 2002 is the Darwin Centre, which will allow visitors to watch scientists at work in laboratories normally hidden from view. There will also be guided tours of the reserve collections of animals, plants and rocks which are too numerous to be displayed in the main galleries.

NATURAL HISTORY MUSEUM, Cromwell Road, London SW7 5BD.

Telephone: 020 7942 5000. Group bookings 020 7942 5555.

Website: www.nhm.ac.uk

Open: Monday to Saturday 10.00–17.50; Sunday 11.00–17.50.

Admission charge. Children aged sixteen and under and senior citizens free. Free for everyone after 16.30 (17.00 weekends). Free for all from December 2001.

Nearest Underground: South Kensington.

Buses: 14, 49, 70, 74, 345, C1.

The **Science Museum** has seven floors dedicated to the history and development of science, with subject sections such as transport, medicine, computers and engineering. There are historical exhibits, working models and lots of hands-on displays aimed at children of all ages – but adults will be just as interested as the children. In 2000 the Wellcome Wing opened at the rear of the museum, demonstrating modern developments in science and technology.

The main interactive area is the **Launch Pad**, where young children are encouraged to take part in a number of experiments to find out how and why things work. There are members of staff on hand to help, and they also give special demonstrations from time to time. In the basement are two more hands-on areas: the Garden is aimed at children aged three to six and Things is for those aged seven to eleven.

The first thing you see as you enter the museum is a display of **steam engines** and turbines, some among the earliest steam engines of the Industrial Revolution. Occasionally they can be seen operating. Beyond is the **Exploration of Space** gallery, with a large assortment of rockets and satellites, a recreation of a moon landing with the Apollo 11 lunar module, and a model of Neil Armstrong becoming the first man to walk on the moon, wearing a life support system on his back.

The **Making the Modern World** display houses a wonderful array of objects from the eighteenth century to the present day representing key moments in scientific and technological development. Here you will find two of the oldest steam locomotives, *Puffing Billy* and the *Rocket,* early cars and bicycles, a lawn-mower of 1832, and domestic appliances such as washing machines and picnic sets. One of the most popular exhibits is the actual Apollo 10 command module that circled the moon in May 1969. Amazingly, three astronauts were squeezed into this small space. Perhaps the most stunning object is the Lockheed Electra airliner from 1935 which hangs dramatically from the ceiling. On the third floor is a gallery dedicated to flight, with many more historic aeroplanes, including the flimsy-looking Vickers Vimy biplane in which Alcock and Brown made the first non-stop flight across the Atlantic in 1919.

At the back of the ground floor is the entrance to the **Wellcome Wing**, with today's developments in science and technology presented using today's technology and lots of interactive displays. Some of the exhibits can be changed at short notice in response to new discoveries. The first floor has an exhibition called 'Who am I?' which looks at how the brain works and what makes us all individuals. On

A visit to the Science Museum is a very hands-on experience.

display is the skeleton of a two-thousand-year-old man and what has been found out about him by scientific analysis. Four of his living relatives have been identified by geneticists. The second floor is occupied by Digitopolis, which is all about computers, and In Future on the top floor asks questions about how life will differ in the years to come. You can also go on a simulated space journey and visit a new IMAX cinema which shows 2D and 3D films on a massive screen, creating images so lifelike you feel you are part of the action. There is an extra charge for these two attractions.

SCIENCE MUSEUM, Exhibition Road, London SW7 2DD.

Telephone: 0870 870 4771. Fax: 020 7942 4302. Education: 020 7942 4777.

Website: www.sciencemuseum.org.uk

Open: daily 10.00–18.00.

Admission charge. Children sixteen and under and senior citizens free. Free to all after 16.30. From December 2001 the museum will be free to all visitors.

Nearest Underground: South Kensington.

Buses: 14, 49, 70, 74, 345, C1.

The **Victoria and Albert Museum**, also known as the V&A, is one of the world's finest museums of the decorative arts. Its collections include sculpture, costume, musical instruments, jewellery, textiles and furniture from all over the world. It is an enormous building, with over 7 miles (more than 11 km) of galleries, so it is advisable to pick up the free plan at the information desk and choose what you want to see (though just wandering around can produce unexpected pleasures). Also available at the information desk are gallery trails and details of special events and activities for children and families. Many changes have taken place in the museum, including the refurbishment of the British galleries (due to reopen in late 2001). If there is anything you specifically want to see, it is worth checking if it is on display. For the future, the museum is hoping to build an extension known as The Spiral, an exciting and controversial building by Daniel Libeskind.

The earliest objects in the museum are in the Medieval Treasury. Here are displayed superb examples of the exquisite handiwork of the Middle Ages, most of it of a religious nature. Look out for the twelfth-century Gloucester Candlestick, which is covered in cavorting men and monsters, and the colourful enamelled **Becket Casket**, which once held relics of Thomas Becket, the Archbishop of Canterbury murdered in his cathedral in 1170; the scene on the front of the box is of the four knights carrying out the murder while Becket is praying.

One of the most popular objects in the museum is **Tipu's Tiger** in the India gallery. It shows a tiger attacking a British soldier, who is lying on the ground trying to protect himself. The tiger's body is, in fact, an organ, and used to make the sound of the roaring tiger and the groans of the soldier. It was made for Tipu, the Sultan of Mysore, and was taken by the British after they captured his capital in 1799.

The **Dress Collection** is one of the finest in the world, with clothes and accessories from the sixteenth century to the present day. Both men and women have often gone to the most extraordinary lengths to be fashionable, even if it meant being uncomfortable. Notice, in particular, the immense width of the women's eighteenth-century mantuas, which must have made it very difficult getting through doors. There are several cases of underwear, including uncomfortable-looking whalebone corsets. The twentieth century is well represented, with mini-skirts from the 1960s and Vivienne Westwood's unmistakable platform shoes.

In a gallery above the Dress Collection is a wonderful assortment of musical instruments collected purely for their design; some of them are brightly painted or intricately carved. The most unusual of all is the aptly named Giraffe Piano, with its huge curved top making it look like an upturned grand piano.

You should not miss the **Raphael Cartoons**, not cartoons as we know them today, but a series of full-sized designs by the great Renaissance painter Raphael for tapestries commissioned by Pope Leo X to hang in the Sistine Chapel in the Vatican. They were bought by Charles I when he was Prince of Wales and are now on

Tipu's Tiger is on display in the India gallery at the Victoria and Albert Museum.

permanent loan to the museum. The best-known painting is *The Miraculous Draught of Fishes*, which shows Christ sitting in a boat helping Peter and the other fishermen fill their boats with fish. On the opposite wall is an English tapestry made from the design, but you will see that it is a mirror image of the original, as the tapestry weavers worked from the back of the loom, reversing the image.

Another popular exhibit is the **Great Bed of Ware**, which dates from about 1580, an enormous four-poster bed, big enough for a large family, and carved from head to foot. It was made as a tourist attraction for the White Hart Inn at Ware in Hertfordshire and is mentioned by Shakespeare in *Twelfth Night*. Also worth finding are the sixteenth-century **Dacre Beasts**, four brightly coloured heraldic animals which used to guard Dacre Castle in Cumbria. At over 6 feet (1.8 metres) tall, they represent a bull, a gryphon, a ram and a salmon with a crown and were all carved from a single oak tree. They are said to have inspired some of the original illustrations for Lewis Carroll's *Alice in Wonderland*.

VICTORIA AND ALBERT MUSEUM, Cromwell Road, London SW7 2RL.

Telephone: 020 7942 2000. Education: 020 7942 2197.

Website: www.vam.ac.uk

Open: Thursday to Tuesday 10.00–17.45; Wednesday 10.00–22.00; last Friday of the month 10.00–22.00.

Admission charge, but free after 16.30. Children under eighteen and senior citizens free. From December 2001 the museum will be free to all visitors.

Nearest Underground: South Kensington.

Buses: 14, 49, 70, 74, 345, C1.

21
Hyde Park and Kensington Gardens

Hyde Park and Kensington Gardens between them form the largest open space in central London. London is famous for its many open spaces and chief among them are the Royal Parks, which are owned by the Crown but open to the public. They were mostly used as hunting parks by the Tudor monarchs but it was under the Stuarts that they took on the appearance they have today. They are places in which to relax or be energetic, depending on your mood.

Hyde Park used to belong to Westminster Abbey; when Henry VIII closed the monasteries he took the land and stocked it with deer and both he and Elizabeth I hunted here. Charles I opened the park to the public and during the reign of Charles II it was a fashionable place to be seen in. When William III lived at Kensington Palace he had lamps hung along the south side of Hyde Park to make his journey safer as the area was frequented by robbers. The road became known as the *Route du Roi* (King's Road), which became corrupted into Rotten Row, now a sandy track popular with horse-riders. The park is also loved by joggers. You can hire a boat on the Serpentine lake or swim in the lido beside it; some hardy souls swim here throughout the year whatever the weather, even on Christmas Day, when they compete for the Peter Pan Cup.

On special occasions such as royal birthdays and state visits a forty-one gun royal salute is fired in Hyde Park by the King's Troop, Royal Horse Artillery, at 12.00 in front of the Dorchester Hotel; if the date falls on a Sunday, the salute takes place on the Monday. The soldiers arrive on horseback in dramatic style pulling the gun carriages behind them (see Chapter 1).

In the north-east corner of the park is **Speakers' Corner**, where every Sunday speakers get on their soapboxes to air their views on any subject under the sun, so long as they do not blaspheme or insult the Queen. It can be interesting and amusing to listen to the various speakers and the banter between them and their hecklers. Nearby is **Marble Arch**, which was originally built by John Nash as a grand

Every Sunday a crowd gathers in Hyde Park to listen to people air their views at Speakers' Corner.

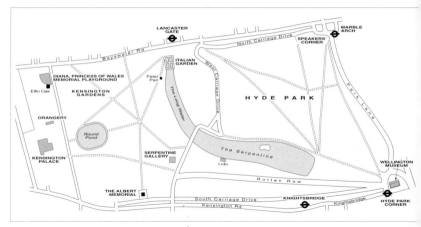

entrance to Buckingham Palace. The arch was later moved here to be an entrance to the park, but unfortunately it is now isolated in the middle of a traffic roundabout. Just to the north of Marble Arch is the site of Tyburn, the infamous gallows where so many people were hanged, often for very minor offences. Up to twenty-one people could be hanged at the same time and an execution day was treated as a public holiday. Thousands of onlookers would line the route from Newgate Prison along Oxford Street to cheer or jeer, and the victims would be offered drinks to help them on their way. For particularly popular hangings, grandstand seats were provided and on several occasions they collapsed, killing a number of spectators.

Kensington Palace was remodelled for William III, who suffered from asthma and needed to move from Whitehall into the country for his health; **Kensington Gardens** were created as the palace's private gardens. Several kings and queens lived in the palace, the last being Victoria, who was born here and lived here until she became queen. Diana, Princess of Wales, lived here and people still leave flowers on the gates where thousands of bouquets piled up in the days after her death in 1997. Several members of the royal family still have apartments in the palace. The state apartments are open to the public but the private rooms are not on view. The palace is not as grand as Buckingham Palace or Hampton Court, but there are some elaborately painted ceilings and a staircase with hundreds of painted figures round the walls. You can visit the room where Victoria lived and the room where she was baptised. There is a special display of ceremonial dress worn at court from the eighteenth century to the present day. You can also see some of the Queen's dresses and a selection of royal children's clothes of the last two hundred years, including the miniature robes worn by the Princesses Elizabeth and Margaret at their father's coronation in 1937. A selection of dresses worn by Diana, Princess of Wales, is also on show. In front of the palace is the delightful Sunken Garden and nearby is the Orangery, where you can have afternoon tea.

KENSINGTON PALACE, Kensington Gardens, London W8 4PX.

Telephone: 020 7937 9561. Fax: 020 7376 0198.

Website: www.hrp.org.uk

Open: March to October, 10.00–18.00; November to February, 10.00–17.00.

Admission charge.

Nearest Underground: Queensway, Notting Hill Gate, High Street Kensington.

Buses: 9, 10, 27, 28, 49, 52, 70, 328.

The pirate ship in the Diana, Princess of Wales Memorial Playground.

Running alongside the palace is the Broad Walk, a wide path much frequented by cyclists and rollerbladers. You may also see members of the Parks police on in-line skates; they have found this is a good way to get around their beat. To the north of

the palace is the **Diana, Princess of Wales Memorial Playground**, which opened in the summer of 2000 as a tribute to the Princess, who was particularly fond of children. It has plenty to keep children occupied and disabled children are also catered for. Its themed areas (such as a pirate ship, wigwams and a tree house) offer lots of variety and have proved enormously successful, with queues forming at peak times. The design of the playground is based on J. M. Barrie's famous book *Peter Pan.* (Barrie lived in a house to the north of the park and funded an earlier playground on the site.) The playground is open from 10.00 and is for children up to the age of twelve. Unaccompanied children or adults are not admitted. By the entrance to the playground is the **Elfin Oak**, with elves, fairies and animals carved into its trunk and painted in

The Elfin Oak in Kensington Gardens.

bright colours. It was originally created in 1930 by Ivor Innes from a tree stump in Richmond Park. Its restoration owes much to the efforts of the comedian Spike Milligan with help from Prince Charles.

Set into the ground near the Elfin Oak is a bronze plaque with a rose at its centre, one of eighty plaques marking the route of the **Diana, Princess of Wales Memorial Walk**, which you can follow round Kensington Gardens, Hyde Park, Green Park and St James's Park. Many of the plaques are close to buildings or locations which are closely associated with the Princess.

There are lots of statues in the park, of which the most popular and charming is **Peter Pan**, which you will find in the north of the park overlooking the Long Water (as the Serpentine is called in Kensington Gardens). The ageless boy plays his flute on top of a mound covered in animals and elves, many of which now shine from the constant rubbing of young hands. J. M. Barrie arranged for the statue to be put up overnight so that it seemed to have appeared as if by magic.

On the south side of the park is one of London's most unusual monuments, the **Albert Memorial**. Erected in memory of Queen Victoria's beloved consort, it is in the form of an enormous medieval shrine and is covered in mosaics, carvings and gold leaf, so that it shimmers and glitters among the trees. Underneath it is the heavily gilded statue of a seated Albert holding a copy of the catalogue of the Great Exhibition of 1851, which he helped organise. The exhibition was held nearby in Hyde Park in a huge iron and glass building called the Crystal Palace; the structure was later moved to Sydenham in south London where, after many years as a popular attraction, it burnt down in 1936. The exhibition was a great success and the profits

went towards the purchase of land to the south of the park where a number of educational establishments were built, including the three museums described in the previous chapter.

Opposite the Albert Memorial is the huge, oval **Royal Albert Hall**. All sorts of events are held here, including sport and opera, but it is best known for the Promenade Concerts which take place here every summer (see Chapter 1).

The Peter Pan statue in Kensington Gardens.

22
Tate Britain

In the late nineteenth century the sugar magnate Sir Henry Tate (the man who invented the sugar cube) gave his collection of British paintings to the nation and they were housed in a newly built art gallery named after him beside the Thames at Millbank. For over a hundred years a growing collection of modern international art hung alongside the national collection in the Tate Gallery. In 2000, the bulk of the modern collection moved downstream to the new Tate Modern at Bankside (see Chapter 25) and the gallery at Millbank, renamed Tate Britain, now displays the most comprehensive collection of British art, including oil paintings, watercolours and sculpture.

The displays are changed regularly and are not arranged chronologically, but thematically, so that you can compare portraits or landscapes from different periods, though major artists may have a room to themselves. There are important works by most of the greatest artists, including Hogarth, Reynolds, Gainsborough, Constable and Turner, as well as twentieth-century artists such as Stanley Spencer and David Hockney. The Pre-Raphaelites are also well represented, with major works by Rossetti, Millais and Burne-Jones. The whole collection is too large to be on display at once, so if there is anything you are particularly keen to see it is worth asking at the information desk under the rotunda. You can also ask here for details of the free guided tours and other activities.

The earliest pictures are from the Tudor period, including Nicholas **Hilliard**'s famous portrait of Queen Elizabeth I wearing a spectacular embroidered dress covered in jewels, all painted in extraordinary detail. Elizabeth was in her forties when the picture was painted, but she looks younger, with a red wig and a smooth, heavily made-up face – this is the flattering goddess-like image of herself she wished to create. A much more realistic portrait is that by **Van Dyck** from the 1630s of an unknown lady of the Spencer family, an ancestor of Diana, Princess of Wales. Van Dyck was the master of flattering portraits and depicting the luxurious silks and satins of the period.

During the eighteenth century the first great British artists came to prominence (before this the best painters had come from elsewhere in Europe). **Hogarth** was both a portrait painter and a satirist and his best-known work combines humour and social comment. In his *O The Roast Beef of Old England* notice the way the fat monk and the French soldiers are eyeing up the succulent joint of meat. Of the eighteenth-century portraits, perhaps the most beautiful is **Gainsborough**'s elegant picture of a dancer, *Giovanna Baccelli*, which is full of movement. There are several paintings by George **Stubbs**, who was famous for his pictures of horses, of which *Mares and Foals in a River Landscape* is a fine example.

From the early nineteenth century there are a number of **Constable** landscapes, including the famous *Flatford Mill*, a scene from his beloved Suffolk, where he was brought up and which he continued to paint throughout his life. A typically realistic picture, it contains the wide range of greens for which he was renowned. The Tate has the finest collection of **Turner**'s work to be found anywhere, covering the whole of his life's work. One of his most impressive early works is *Snow Storm: Hannibal and His Army Crossing the Alps*, which shows his life-long interest in storms. See if you can spot the tiny elephant on the horizon. Turner was also fascinated by the sea and there are many dramatic seascapes on display.

One of the most unusual pictures in the gallery is the finely detailed *The Fairy Teller's Master Stroke* by Richard Dadd. It depicts a scene from Shakespeare's

Midsummer Night's Dream, with all the tiny fairy folk amongst the tall grass and the giant daisies, and was painted while Dadd was locked up in an asylum after he had killed his father.

Some of the most popular pictures in the gallery are by the **Pre-Raphaelites**, with their brilliant colours and exquisite detail. Millais spent nearly four months in Surrey painting from life the background to his *Ophelia*, who is shown drowned in a river covered in lots of clearly identifiable flowers. The model posed in a bath of water kept warm by lamps; when on one occasion they went out, she caught a very bad chill.

Towards the end of the nineteenth century many artists were influenced by the French Impressionists. One of the loveliest pictures of this type is **John Singer Sargent**'s *Carnation, Lily, Lily, Rose*, of two young girls with Chinese lanterns at dusk surrounded by flowers.

The twentieth-century collection includes examples by most of the important British artists, including paintings by Stanley Spencer, Francis Bacon, Lucien Freud and David Hockney, sculpture by Barbara Hepworth and Henry Moore, and installations by more recent artists. The modern collection of British art is shared between Tate Britain and the Tate Modern gallery, so to complete the story you will need to make a trip to Bankside (see Chapter 25).

TATE BRITAIN, Millbank, London SW1P 4RG.

Telephone: 020 7887 8008.

Website: www.tate.org.uk

Admission free, except for special exhibitions.

Open: daily 10.00–17.50.

Nearest Underground: Pimlico.

Buses: 2, 3, 36, 77A, 88, 185, 507, C10.

The Imperial War Museum.

23
The Imperial War Museum

The Imperial War Museum is devoted to telling the stories of wars since 1914, especially those that have involved British troops, but in no way does it glorify war. The museum is housed in a building which for most of the nineteenth century was the Bethlem Hospital, a mental institution more commonly called Bedlam. (The only bedlam now is the result of the many school groups enjoying a visit!) The main focus of the collections is the **First** and **Second World Wars**, but more recent conflicts such as the **Falklands War** and the **Gulf War** are also included. The story

The Holocaust Exhibition at the Imperial War Museum.

is presented using real tanks and aircraft, films and diaries, showing how those at the front or at home were affected by war. Regular special exhibitions and lots of activities are organised for children.

In front of the main entrance are two enormous guns from First World War battleships, each weighing 100 tons. The first things you see in the large central area inside the museum are more of the larger exhibits, including tanks, aircraft, bombs and guns from both world wars. Above are British **aeroplanes**, including a Sopwith Camel from 1918 and a Spitfire from the Battle of Britain, and German aircraft such as a Heinkel. Also on display are a massive V2 guided ballistic missile, many thousands of which fell on London during the Second World War, and a Polaris missile from the 1960s. You can also see the *Tamzine*, a 14 foot (4.3 metre) fishing boat, the smallest of the many 'little ships' involved in the evacuation of Dunkirk in 1940. In the centre of the hall is, rather unexpectedly, an old London bus: nicknamed **Ole Bill**, it was used at the front in the First World War when the army was short of vehicles.

Up on the first floor are more large exhibits, including the cockpit section of a Lancaster bomber. Also on this level is a display on the **Secret War**, examining the world of espionage and the work of MI5 and MI6. Here you will find bottles of invisible ink, codebooks and an original German Enigma encoding machine. On the second floor are galleries devoted to the art of the two world wars, including *Gassed*, a powerful depiction by John Singer Sargent of groups of soldiers temporarily blinded by gas being led to safety.

In the basement the stories of the two world wars are told in greater detail, describing what life was like for those at home as well as those fighting at the front. On display are documents, weapons, uniforms, medals and personal effects, and screens show newsreel footage. Part of the First World War section is the **Trench Experience**, a recreation, with special sound effects and smells, of a trench at the Somme in 1916, though fortunately without the mud. The **Blitz Experience**, in the Second World War area, uses similar techniques to enable you to feel as if you have been caught in the London Blitz of 1940. One part of the experience is sitting in a draughty bunker while mock bombs go off all around you; there can be queues on busy days.

The **Holocaust** exhibition tells the harrowing stories of the mass extermination by the Nazis of Jews and other groups during the Second World War and other genocides with the aid of photographs, letters, diaries, newspapers and everyday objects. Among the most moving items are a pile of shoes and a funeral cart from the Warsaw Ghetto. The stories of some of those who survived the Holocaust are also told.

IMPERIAL WAR MUSEUM, Lambeth Road, London SE1 6HZ.

Telephone: 020 7416 5000. Recorded information: 09001 600 140.

Website: www.iwm.org.uk

Open: daily 10.00–18.00.

Admission charge, but free for all after 16.30. Senior citizens and children under sixteen free.

Nearest Underground: Lambeth North, Elephant & Castle, Waterloo.

Buses: 1, 3, 12, 45, 53, 63, 68, 100, 159, 168, 171, 172, 176, 188, 344, C10.

24
South Bank walk

It is now possible to walk along the south side of the river Thames all the way from Westminster Bridge to Tower Bridge. There are many interesting attractions to visit, some new, some old, and as the whole walk is rather long, it has been broken up into three shorter sections. In this chapter we cover the section from Westminster to Blackfriars Bridge (see Chapter 25 for Bankside and Chapter 26 for London Bridge to Tower Bridge).

The walk starts at Westminster Underground station. First cross to Westminster Bridge, passing the dramatic statue of **Boudicca**, queen of the Iceni tribe who led a violent revolt against the Roman rulers in AD 60. From the bridge there are excellent views in both directions, to the right the Houses of Parliament, with the clock tower in the foreground, and to the left the Thames curving away towards the City. The whole view is dominated by the unmistakable shape of the British Airways London Eye observation wheel.

Cross the bridge to the south side, where you will find the statue of the **South Bank Lion**. It is made of Coade stone, a waterproof artificial stone much used to decorate London's buildings in the eighteenth and nineteenth centuries. Unfortunately, the formula has since been lost. On the other side of the bridge is St Thomas's Hospital, where in the nineteenth century Florence Nightingale created her famous nursing school (see Chapter 28). Steps lead down to a walkway alongside the river in front of County Hall, the headquarters of London's govern-

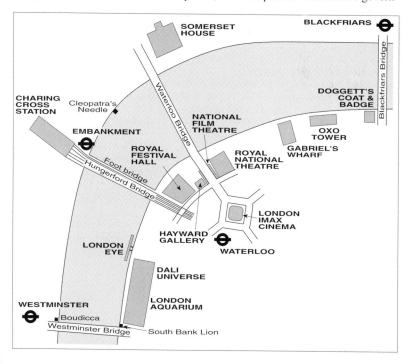

At the London Aquarium you can watch the sharks or for a more hands-on experience you can stroke the rays in the Beach Pool.

ment until the Greater London Council was abolished in 1986. It now houses flats, hotels and several attractions.

The **London Aquarium** is home to a wide variety of fish and other aquatic creatures from all round the world. There are lots of themed areas, such as mangrove swamps and rainforests, with appropriate background noises to give the right atmosphere. Huge three-storey tanks representing the Atlantic and Pacific Oceans introduce you to eels, stingrays and sharks. Elsewhere you can see delicate seahorses, poisonous lionfish and a tankful of piranha, which grow frenzied at feeding times. Get your hands wet in the Seashore, where you are allowed to hold starfish and anemones, and you can stroke the friendly rays in the Beach Pool.

LONDON AQUARIUM, County Hall, London SE1 7PB.

Telephone: 020 7967 8000. Fax: 020 7967 8029.

Website: www.londonaquarium.co.uk

Open: daily 10.00–18.00.

Admission charge.

Nearest Underground: Westminster, Waterloo.

Buses: 12, 53, 77, 159, 211, 381, 507.

A little further on some curious sculptures announce the **Dalí Universe**, an exhibition of the work of the famous Spanish surrealist artist Salvador Dalí. The collection includes sculpture, watercolours, prints and some brightly coloured glass

The view of the South Bank from the London Eye.

sculptures. Many of the images, such as melting clocks and long-legged elephants, are familiar from his better-known paintings, but there are also some highly original objects on display, including jewellery and a sofa in the shape of Mae West's lips. This exhibition may be more suitable for families with older children.

DALI UNIVERSE, County Hall, London SE1 7PB.
Telephone: 020 7620 2720.
Website: www.daliuniverse.com
Open: daily 10.00–17.30.
Admission charge.
Nearest Underground: Westminster, Waterloo.
Buses: 12, 53, 77, 159, 211, 381, 507.

You will now be standing right underneath the British Airways **London Eye**, which, since it opened in 2000, has become one of London's most popular attractions. At 450 feet (135 metres) it is the fourth highest structure in London and

offers spectacular views over the capital. Its construction aroused great interest, with all the sections arriving by river and the enormous structure being assembled on islands built out over the Thames, and there was an anxious moment when technical problems left the wheel suspended half way up. The trip lasts about half an hour and the wheel moves slowly enough for you to wander round the glass capsule taking in the breathtaking sights. Although you do not need

The London Imax Cinema near Waterloo station.

to book, it may be advisable to reserve tickets for busier periods such as weekends and holidays.

BRITISH AIRWAYS LONDON EYE, South Bank, London SE1 7PB.

Telephone: 0870 5000 600 (automated booking line).

Website: www.british-airways.com/londoneye

Open: summer 10.00–22.00; winter 10.00–19.00 (times may vary).

Admission charge.

Nearest Underground: Westminster, Waterloo.

Buses: 12, 53, 77, 159, 211, 381, 507.

Continuing your walk alongside the river, you pass under a railway bridge and come out by the **Royal Festival Hall**. Built in 1951 for the Festival of Britain, it is now part of the South Bank Centre. It is one of London's main concert halls and offers a variety of classical, folk, jazz and dance programmes, as well as special concerts for children. In the large foyer are cafes and shops and there is free music at lunchtime. Also in the South Bank Centre are two smaller concert halls and the Hayward Gallery, which holds regular art exhibitions. This stretch of the river is very popular with rollerbladers and skateboarders, especially in the spaces under the buildings.

SOUTH BANK CENTRE, London SE1 8XX.

Bookings: 020 7960 4242.

Website: www.sbc.org.uk

Nearest Underground: Waterloo, Embankment.

Buses: 1, 4, 26, 59, 68, 76, 77, 168, 171, 172, 176, 188, 341, 501, 521.

Looking back over the river you can see, to the left, the striking modern arch-shaped Embankment Place, built over the top of Charing Cross station. Further right is the Shell-Mex building, with London's largest clock-face. Right in the middle is **Cleopatra's Needle**, an Egyptian obelisk which actually has nothing to do with Cleopatra but was given by the Viceroy of Egypt and put up here in 1878. A time capsule was buried underneath with newspapers, coins, a railway timetable and a picture of Queen Victoria.

Under Waterloo Bridge is an open-air book market and the **National Film Theatre**, which has three cinemas offering a wide range of classic and new films. There are sometimes junior matinees at weekends.

NATIONAL FILM THEATRE, South Bank, London SE1 8YY.

Telephone: 020 7633 0274.

Website: www.bfi.org.uk

Nearest Underground: Waterloo, Embankment.

Buses: 1, 4, 26, 59, 68, 76, 77, 168, 171, 172, 176, 188, 341, 501, 521.

Nearby is the **London Imax Cinema**, built in the centre of a traffic roundabout in front of Waterloo Station. It has one of the biggest screens in Europe, ten storeys high, and shows both 2D and 3D films, which make you feel as if you are part of the action.

LONDON IMAX CINEMA, South Bank, London SE1 8XR.

Telephone: 020 7902 1234.

Website: www.bfi.org.uk

Admission charge.

Open: 12.00–22.00.

Nearest Underground: Waterloo.

Buses: 1, 4, 26, 59, 68, 76, 77, 168, 171, 172, 176, 188, 501, 507, 521.

Beyond Waterloo Bridge is the **Royal National Theatre**, one of London's major subsidised theatres. It actually contains three separate theatres and offers a wide range of plays, both classical and modern. They often put on plays aimed at a family audience, especially at Christmas, so it is worth checking the current programme. It is also possible to go on a backstage tour to see just how much hard work goes into creating the final production.

ROYAL NATIONAL THEATRE, South Bank, London, SE1 9PX.

Telephone: 020 7452 3400 (information and backstage tours).

Website: www.nt-online.org

Nearest Underground: Waterloo, Embankment.

Buses: 1, 4, 26, 59, 68, 76, 77, 168, 171, 172, 176, 188, 341, 501, 502.

A little further along a panel identifies all the buildings you can see on the other side of the Thames. To the left, alongside Waterloo Bridge, is **Somerset House**, which houses the Inland Revenue but is also home to three galleries including the Courtauld Institute Galleries and the Gilbert Collection (see Chapter 10). To the right are the Inner and Middle Temples, two of the historic Inns of Court, where barristers have their chambers.

Walking on, you will notice stairs leading down to the water. These would once have been used by watermen to pick up and drop off passengers in the days when the Thames was London's high street and most people travelled by water. On the right is **Gabriel's Wharf**, a colourful craft market with several eating places. Ahead of you is the **Oxo Tower**, once used as a warehouse by the makers of the famous gravy cubes, who cleverly got round the ban on advertising along the river by making the upper windows spell out the name of their product. The building has been restored and now houses apartments, craft workshops, restaurants and a public viewing gallery on the eighth floor with fine views over London.

Just before Blackfriars Bridge is the Doggett's Coat and Badge pub. It is named after the boat race started in 1715 by the actor-manager Thomas Doggett to celebrate the anniversary of the accession of George I (see Chapter 1). Even today, at the end of July, teams of young watermen dress up in their colourful livery and race the $4^1/_2$ miles (7 km) from London Bridge to Cadogan Pier in Chelsea. The winner is presented with a special red coat and a large silver badge.

You could finish the walk here and cross Blackfriars Bridge to Blackfriars Underground station. Alternatively, you could walk through the subway under the bridge and follow the Bankside walk described in the next chapter.

The new Millennium Bridge and the Tate Modern.

25
Bankside walk

This continues the walk from Westminster Bridge described in the previous chapter and takes you along an historic stretch of the riverside which has been revived by several new developments. The walk begins at Blackfriars, named after the black-robed Dominican friars who had a monastery here in the Middle Ages. Leaving Blackfriars Underground station, turn left on to Blackfriars Bridge. The statue of Queen Victoria commemorates her opening of the bridge in 1869. Between the road bridge and the railway bridge to the left you can see the bright red supports from the first railway bridge. This was built in 1864 for the London, Chatham & Dover Railway, whose colourful insignia can be seen on the other side of the river. In the middle of the road on the south side of the bridge is a dragon, which tells you that you have now left the City of London and are entering Southwark.

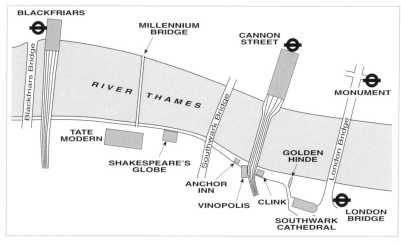

The stage at Shakespeare's Globe Theatre.

After crossing the bridge, take the steps down on the left, turn right at the bottom and walk under the railway bridge. You are now on **Bankside**, an area which was once the main entertainment area of London, where Londoners would come for its theatres, bear-baiting, inns and brothels. There were also a number of prisons here, and smelly industries such as breweries and tanneries operated here, far enough away from the city not to upset its inhabitants, unless the wind was in the wrong direction. The Founders' Arms pub is on the site of the bell foundry which made the bells for St Paul's Cathedral, whose dome can be seen towering above the other buildings across the river. There is a panel a little way past the pub which identifies the main buildings and will help identify some of the City churches which can be spied among the modern buildings.

You will by now have a clear view of the **Millennium Bridge**, the pedestrian bridge which opened in June 2000 (only to close three days later because of an unexpected wobble). Designed by Norman Foster, it was built low over the river to look like a 'blade of light' and at night it does look like that, as it has lights along both sides. It is a very elegant bridge, built to enable people to walk from St Paul's Cathedral across the river to Bankside. Structural alterations were made during 2001 to counteract the wobble and enable the bridge to reopen.

The massive brick building on this side of the river used to be Bankside power station, which supplied electricity to much of central London. After it was decommissioned, £134 million was spent on turning it into **Tate Modern,** a gallery of modern art, opened by the Queen in May 2000. The main brick shell of the old building was kept, but the inside has been rebuilt and an extra glass storey added on top of the structure. The old machinery was removed, although there is a reminder of its former use from the humming of a switching station which has remained. The sheer size of the space of the old turbine hall cannot fail to impress, though the sculptures displayed here are made to look small. The main galleries have been created at the front of the building, so as you walk around you occasionally get views across the Thames. The displays are arranged thematically, enabling you to compare the work of artists from different decades, though some artists have rooms devoted to their work. There is work by Picasso, Matisse, Dalí, Stanley Spencer and Henry Moore as well as more recent work by young British and international artists. As well as paintings and sculpture, there are lots of installations, videos and photographs. There are a number of free guided tours of the collection every day. A trip to the top floor gives you stunning panoramic views out over London.

TATE MODERN, Bankside, London SE1 9TG.

Telephone: 020 7887 8008.

Website: www.tate.org.uk

Open: Sunday to Thursday 10.00–18.00; Friday to Saturday 10.00–22.00.

Admission free, except for special exhibitions.

Nearest Underground: Southwark, Blackfriars, London Bridge.

Buses: 45, 63, 100, 381, 344.

A little further on there is a short row of old houses. Legend has it that Sir Christopher Wren lived in the one with the plaque; from there he was able to watch his new St Paul's Cathedral going up. By now you will have caught glimpses of a half-timbered building with a thatched roof. This is **Shakespeare's Globe**, a reconstruction of the Globe Theatre which opened here in 1599 and where many of Shakespeare's plays were first performed. It has been built as closely as possible to the original design with the techniques used for the original, although as modern safety standards have had to be followed, there are sprinklers sticking up out of the thatch. The wood is oak, the walls are of lath and plaster, and the roof is thatched with reed. The gates on the river side are rather striking, as they depict animals, birds and plants mentioned in Shakespeare's plays, including a crab, a mermaid and various monsters.

The main entrance is round the corner in New Globe Walk. Here you can join a guided tour of the building and learn about its construction and how it works as a theatre, with its tiers of wooden galleries surrounding an open space that has a stage on one side. Coming to a performance here is unlike a trip to a modern theatre: there is no proscenium arch and little scenery, and the actors can see the audience, giving a more intimate feeling. All plays used to be performed during daylight hours, but today there are special lights which create a daylight effect for evening perform-ances. In Shakespeare's day people would eat and drink during the performance, and they would hiss and cheer the actors. Even today there is more audience participa-tion than in other theatres. The cheapest tickets are for the 'groundlings', who stand in the central area, which is open to the elements, and so if it rains they get wet. The stage is covered, protecting the actors and allowing the show to go on in all weathers. For a few pounds more, you can sit in one of the galleries, although the wooden benches are hard (cushions can be hired). As the theatre is open-air it can only be used in the summer, but a second, indoor, theatre is being built for winter performances.

Included in the price of a tour is a visit to a superb exhibition which tells you all about the theatre in Shakespeare's day and about how this replica was built. There are costumes and props from current productions, and touch-screen computers to find out more about how plays were put on in Shakespeare's time. For example, you can learn about special effects, such as trapdoors, flying and hangings. There is a display of Elizabethan musical instruments, including bagpipes, cornetts, sackbuts and crumhorns, complete with demonstrations. Elsewhere you can record yourself in scenes with real actors and edit famous speeches, taking home a printed copy of your version.

SHAKESPEARE'S GLOBE, New Globe Walk, Bankside, London SE1 9DT.

Telephone: 020 7902 1500. Fax: 020 7902 1515. Box office: 020 7401 9919.

Website: www.shakespeares-globe.org

Open: May to September, 9.00–12.00 exhibition and tour, 13.00–16.00 exhibition only; October to April 10.00–17.00 exhibition and tour.

continued opposite

> Admission charge.
> Nearest Underground: London Bridge, Mansion House, Southwark.
> Buses: 45, 63, 100, 344, 381.

Continue along Bankside, passing under Southwark Bridge, and you will soon come to the **Anchor Inn**. This is an historic eighteenth-century pub built on the site of an earlier one which was probably known to Shakespeare. It is a good place for families as there is an outdoor terrace overlooking the river. The next bridge is Cannon Street railway bridge. Under the railway arches is a new attraction called **Vinopolis**, which tells the story of wine from Roman times to the present day. There are imaginative displays on the wines of all the main wine-making regions of Europe and the New World. Included in the admission price is the opportunity to taste five wines (children are offered fruit juice and an activity book).

> VINOPOLIS, 1 Bank End, London SE1.
> Telephone: 0870 241 4040.
> Website: www.vinopolis.co.uk
> Open: Tuesday to Friday and Sunday 11.00–18.00; Saturday 11.00–20.00; Monday 11.00–21.00.
> Admission charge.
> Nearest Underground: London Bridge.
> Buses: 17, 21, 35, 40, 43, 47, 48, 133, 149, 343, 344, 381, 501, 521.

Now walk under the railway bridge into Clink Street, where you will find the **Clink Exhibition**, a small museum on the site of the old Clink Prison, which is the origin of the expression 'in the clink'. The museum has a small display of instruments of torture and tableaux showing what life was like in the prison.

> CLINK EXHIBITION, 1 Clink Street, London SE1 9DG.
> Telephone: 020 7403 6515.
> Website: www.clink.co.uk
> Open: April to August 10.00–22.00; September to March 10.00–18.00.
> Admission charge.
> Nearest Underground: London Bridge.
> Buses: 17, 21, 35, 40, 43, 47, 48, 133, 149, 343, 344, 381, 501, 521.

The Clink was the Bishop of Winchester's private prison and a short walk between old warehouses will bring you to the remains of his medieval palace. Soon you will come to the **_Golden Hinde_**, a replica of the ship in which Sir Francis Drake sailed around the world in the sixteenth century. It may seem too small to be capable of such a feat, but it is a full-scale reconstruction and has itself sailed round the world, travelling more than 140,000 miles (225,000 km) since it was launched in 1973. The ship was made using traditional materials and methods, and a visit gives a very good idea of the cramped and unpleasant conditions endured by the crew. Today's crew, dressed in Elizabethan costume, will tell you all about life aboard the ship. School groups can even spend a night aboard, dressing in sixteenth-century costume and acting out the parts of the crew members.

GOLDEN HINDE, St Mary Overie Dock, London SE1 9DE.
Telephone: 0870 0118 700. Fax: 020 7407 5908.
Website: www.goldenhinde.co.uk
Open: daily 10.00–17.00, but telephone to check.
Admission charge.
Nearest Underground: London Bridge.
Buses: 17, 21, 35, 40, 43, 47, 48, 133, 149, 343, 344, 381, 501, 521.

Walk up Cathedral Street and you will see gates leading to **Southwark Cathedral**, once the parish church of what was London's first suburb. Although much restored, it still retains many fine medieval details. Shakespeare may have worshipped here while he was working at the Globe Theatre and his brother, Edmund, is buried here. Although Shakespeare is buried in his home town of Stratford-upon-Avon, there is a memorial to him, and a stained-glass window depicts many characters from his plays. There is a chapel named after John Harvard, famous for his association with Harvard University. He was born in Southwark and baptised in the church. He became a clergyman and emigrated to Massachusetts, where he died of consumption, leaving money and books to a new college there, which was named after him and is now world famous.

At the west end of the cathedral a door leads to a visitor centre which houses a shop, a cafe and an exhibition called the Long View of London. This small but informative display tells the history of the cathedral and the surrounding area, using touch-screen computers and a number of historic objects, including Roman coins and a fifteenth-century wooden statue from the chapel that stood at the centre of old London Bridge. Interactive cameras that have been mounted on top of the cathedral tower allow you to see a panoramic view of London which you can compare with the same view from past centuries.

SOUTHWARK CATHEDRAL, Montague Close, London SE1 9DA.
Telephone: 020 7637 6700.
Website: dswark.org/cathedral
Cathedral open: daily 8.00–18.00. Admission free.
Exhibition open: Monday to Saturday 10.00–18.00; Sunday 11.00–17.00. Admission charge.
Nearest Underground: London Bridge.
Buses: 17, 21, 35, 40, 43, 47, 48, 133, 149, 343, 344, 381, 501, 521.

After leaving the cathedral, turn right and right again to pass under **London Bridge**. Just after the bridge, climb the steps on the right, which will bring you out on to London Bridge. Walk to the centre of the bridge for a magnificent view, downstream to Tower Bridge and the Tower of London. This is the Upper Pool and once bristled with hundreds of sailing ships bringing tea, coffee and other products into London. In its heyday you could cross the river by stepping from one ship to the next. Now, apart from the occasional barge and sightseeing boat, the only vessel to be seen is HMS *Belfast*. You may like to continue the walk (see Chapter 26) or you can finish it here. The nearest Underground stations are Monument on the north side or London Bridge on the south.

HMS Belfast is moored near London Bridge and is now a museum.

26
London Bridge to Tower Bridge

Start the walk at London Bridge Underground station. First you may like to visit the Southwark Information Centre, which is on the corner of London Bridge and Tooley Street, easily identified from the stone needle above it. Here you can find out more about the historic area of Southwark and its attractions.

Further down Tooley Street is the **London Dungeon**, which graphically illustrates the gruesome aspects of Britain's history, with displays depicting torture, punishment and murder. It is not recommended for those of a nervous disposition or young children, though teenagers almost invariably love it. It is all underneath the arches of London Bridge station and the vibrations from passing trains add to the atmosphere. You can see hangings, garrottings and people being boiled, learn about life in the infamous Newgate Prison, and hear the grisly tale of Jack the Ripper. Some of the exhibits move and a few of the figures talk. There is also a water ride on the River of Death and a Great Fire of London exhibit.

LONDON DUNGEON, Tooley Street, London SE1 2SZ.

Telephone: 020 7403 7221.

Website: www.thedungeons.com

Open: April to September 10.00–18.30; October to March 10.00–17.30 (late night openings July and August).

Admission charge.

Nearest Underground: London Bridge.

Buses: 17, 21, 35, 40, 43, 47, 48, 133, 149, 343, 381, 501, 521.

Further along Tooley Street is the **Britain at War Experience**, a theme museum about life in London during the Second World War. A number of scenes are cleverly

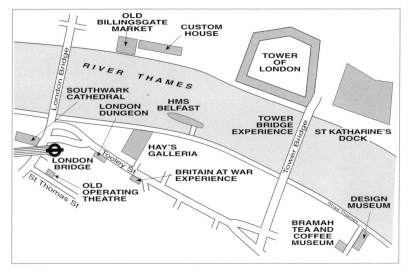

recreated, such as people sleeping in an Underground shelter, a BBC radio studio and a bombed-out street. You can also sit in an Anderson shelter and listen to an air raid going on outside. The walls are decorated with posters, newspapers and magazines of the period and appropriate music is played.

BRITAIN AT WAR EXPERIENCE, 64–66 Tooley Street, London SE1 2TF.
Telephone: 020 7403 3171. Fax: 020 7403 5104.
Website: www.britainatwar.co.uk
Open: April to September 10.00–17.30; October to March 10.00–16.30.
Admission charge.
Nearest Underground: London Bridge.
Buses: 17, 21, 35, 40, 43, 47, 48, 133, 149, 343, 381, 501, 521.

Cross Tooley Street to **Hay's Galleria**, which was once a dock where tea clippers unloaded their cargo. The area became known as 'London's larder' because of the tea, coffee and butter which used to arrive here. The dock has been restored and covered with a glass roof and now houses a range of shops, craft stalls and restaurants. The centrepiece is an inventive sculpture, 'The Navigators', which occasionally comes alive and spouts water. At the Tooley Street end is a shop which sells Christmas gifts and decorations all year round.

From the riverside walk you get a good view of the City across the river, with its mixture of old and modern buildings. The small brick building to the right of the modern blue glass building was Billingsgate Market, where Londoners went to buy their fresh fish. It has been refurbished for use as offices and the fish market has moved to Docklands. The big stone building to the right is Custom House, where duty from all the anchored ships was collected. Customs and Excise still operate from here.

The large ship moored here is **HMS *Belfast***, a cruiser that played an important role in the Second World War and later in Korea. She is now permanently moored here as a museum. A number of well-mounted displays tell the story of the part she played in the conflicts. All seven decks can be visited, from the bridge to the boiler room, and you can see the cramped living quarters, the galley, the sickbay and the punishment cell. You can even operate the Bofors guns. But be warned – there are a lot of ladders to be climbed.

HMS *BELFAST*, Morgans Lane, London SE1 2JH.
Telephone: 020 7940 6300. Fax: 020 7403 0719.
Website: www.hmsbelfast.org.uk
Open: March to October 10.00–18.00; November to February 10.00–17.00.
Admission charge.
Nearest Underground: London Bridge.
Buses: 42, 47, 78, 381.

The riverside walk continues all the way to Tower Bridge, past the site of the headquarters of the first elected Mayor of London. This amazing steel and glass structure, looking a bit like a fencing helmet, has been designed by Norman Foster and is due to be ready in 2002. The walkway takes you under the approach to Tower Bridge and into Shad Thames, a narrow street between tall warehouses, with high bridges between them. Here are a number of shops and restaurants and two specialist museums, which may be of interest to families with older children.

The **Design Museum** has a small permanent collection and mounts changing exhibitions on a number of different topics. It aims to explain why objects such as kettles, washing machines and cars look as they do, highlighting the functional and aesthetic aspects.

DESIGN MUSEUM, Butlers Wharf, 28 Shad Thames, London SE1 2YD.
Telephone: 020 7403 6933. Fax: 020 7378 6540.
Website: www.designmuseum.org.
Open: Monday to Friday 11.30–18.00; Saturday to Sunday 10.30–18.00.
Admission charge.
Nearest Underground: London Bridge, Tower Hill.
Buses: 42, 47, 78, 188, 225, 381.

The **Bramah Tea and Coffee Museum** is one of London's more unusual museums. It tells the story of our two favourite drinks from their introduction to London in the seventeenth century. There is an extensive collection of over a thousand teapots and coffee makers, many in the most unusual shapes.

BRAMAH TEA AND COFFEE MUSEUM, 1 Maguire Street, London SE1 2NQ.
Telephone: 020 7378 0222.
Website: www.bramahmuseum.co.uk
Open: daily 10.00–18.00.
Admission charge.
Travel details as for Design Museum.

From here you can either return to London Bridge station or cross Tower Bridge to Tower Hill station.

The market held in Covent Garden is one of London's most popular shopping areas (see Chapter 11).

27
Street markets

There is more to shopping in London than Oxford Street, Regent Street and Knightsbridge. Shopping in street markets is becoming increasingly popular and London has lots of very different markets catering for all tastes, from traditional general markets selling fresh fruit and vegetables to those that sell fashionable clothes at reasonable prices. Markets have become so popular that unfortunately you do need to look after your valuables, as pickpockets usually follow the crowds.

Berwick Street
In central London the best of the traditional markets is in Berwick Street, right in the heart of Soho, where there has been a market since the middle of the nineteenth century. It sells a wide range of good quality fruit and vegetables, including much exotic produce, and there are also stalls where you can buy cheese and fresh bread. Berwick Street is a good place to look around and maybe buy a picnic lunch.

> BERWICK STREET MARKET, London W1.
>
> Open: Monday to Saturday 9.00–17.00.
>
> Nearest Underground: Piccadilly Circus.
>
> Buses: 38, 19, 14.

Portobello Road
The most famous place in London to buy antiques is Portobello Road Market in Notting Hill, now one of the most fashionable areas in which to live in London. Portobello Market is actually several markets. During the week there is only a

general market, but the best day to go is a Saturday, when the antiques market is operating as well. There are plenty of food outlets along the full length of the market.

From Notting Hill Gate Underground station it is about ten minutes walk to the beginning of the market, but you will have no problem finding it – just follow the crowds. The main antiques market is a mixture of shops and stalls lining both sides of the road, which can get very narrow in places. There are lots of specialist shops offering jewellery, china or clothing, but there are also more unexpected wares on offer, such as fossils, gas masks and Beatles memorabilia. As the market is now very much a tourist attraction, there are even a number of shops selling London souvenirs.

Further up the road is the general market, selling fruit and vegetables, flowers, fish and cheap clothes. The top end, after the flyover, is more of a market for second-hand goods. It is a lot quieter than the other end and has fewer tourists, but some of the best places to eat can be found here. If you do get this far, Ladbroke Grove Tube station is closer than Notting Hill Gate.

PORTOBELLO ROAD MARKET, London W11.

Open: general market Monday to Saturday 9.00–17.00; antiques market Saturday 8.00–17.30.

Website: www.portobelloroad.co.uk

Nearest Underground: Notting Hill Gate, Ladbroke Grove.

Buses: 12, 27, 28, 31, 52, 70, 94, 328.

Petticoat Lane

The best known of London's Sunday markets is Petticoat Lane, which rather confusingly takes place in and around Middlesex Street. There has been a market here since the eighteenth century specialising in second-hand clothes. Its popular name reflects the clothes trade, which is still the main feature of the market, though now the clothes are new. Today the market lives on its reputation as a 'cockney' market and there are hundreds of stalls selling shirts, ties, dresses and underwear at ridiculous prices, though the clothes are not the latest fashions. There are also plenty of bargains to be found on the stalls selling shoes, CDs and jewellery. It is a big, crowded, noisy market, spreading out into the neighbouring streets and with many traders enthusiastically demonstrating their wares with an entertaining sales patter.

PETTICOAT LANE MARKET, Middlesex Street, London E1.

Open: Sunday 9.00–14.00.

Nearest Underground: Liverpool Street, Aldgate, Aldgate East.

Buses: 8, 25, 26, 35, 42, 43, 47, 48, 78, 100, 149, 242, 344.

Spitalfields

Only a few minutes walk from Petticoat Lane is Spitalfields Market, which also operates on Sunday but is far less crowded and more up-market. It is not actually a street market as it is held inside the buildings of an old fruit and vegetable market that closed in 1991, but it has the atmosphere of an outdoor market and in bad weather has the advantage of being under cover. On offer is a great variety of handmade goods, including candles, soaps, paintings and children's clothes. There is a special area selling all sorts of organic food and a food court with booths offering appetising snacks from all round the world.

> SPITALFIELDS MARKET, London E1.
> Open: Sunday 11.00–15.00.
> Nearest Underground: Liverpool Street.
> Buses: 8, 26, 35, 43, 47, 48, 78, 149, 242, 344.

Camden Lock

London's most popular weekend market is Camden Lock Market, especially with young people looking for inexpensive fashion and music. The whole area is so busy that you are not allowed to leave from Camden Town Tube station until after 17.30. It is not just one market, but several, and there are lots of trendy shops up the High Street as well. If you are not keen on crowds, you could visit during the week when some of the stalls are open, but you will miss experiencing the market at its bustling best.

Walking up Camden High Street, you first come to Camden Market, where tightly packed stalls offer a variety of trendy clothes at very reasonable prices. There are boutiques on both sides of the High Street and everywhere loud music fills the air.

Further up the street you come to a bridge over the Regent's Canal. Turn down to the left to walk alongside the canal, from where you get a good view of the delightful setting of Camden Lock Market on the opposite bank, which can be reached via the footbridge. The market covers a huge area, with stalls in and around a complex of buildings that were once the stables and warehouses of a timber yard that relied on the canal for transporting its timber. Now it is a lively market selling a fascinating array of goods, including didgeridoos, second-hand books, beads, mirrors, T-shirts and wood carvings, a good place to browse or pick up an unusual present. There are plenty of places to eat, with food from many different countries.

You could take a short trip along the Regent's Canal from the market to London Zoo in a traditional narrowboat. The service runs hourly, daily in summer and at weekends in winter.

> CAMDEN LOCK MARKET, London NW1.
> Open: Saturday to Sunday 10.00–18.00 (some shops and stalls open during the week).
> Website: www.camdenlock.net
> Nearest Underground: Camden Town.
> Buses: 24, 27, 29, 88, 134, 168, 214, 253, 274, C2.

28
Other places to visit

This chapter describes a number of attractions not covered elsewhere in the book, some of them being a little off the beaten track. Several are of a specialist nature, but all are worth a visit if the subject interests you.

BETHNAL GREEN MUSEUM OF CHILDHOOD

The Bethnal Green Museum of Childhood is quite small and little known, but it is one of London's most delightful museums. It has an excellent collection of toys and dolls and is sure to delight adults as much as children. The collection covers objects from the seventeenth century to the present day from all over the world. As well as the permanent displays there are lots of special exhibitions, and children's events are organised throughout the year.

The toy section includes traditional toys such as rocking horses, toy soldiers, train sets and soft toys, including a wonderful display of early teddy bears. There are also puppets from Burma, India and China, a massive eighteenth-century marionette theatre from Venice and a Punch and Judy show from 1912. Among other exotic items is a beautiful model of a Chinese rock garden made of wood, ivory, jewels and kingfisher feathers. It was intended as a gift to Napoleon's Empress Josephine, but it was captured by British ships before it reached her.

The comprehensive collection of dolls is arranged chronologically to show how they developed from the early stiff figures to the more realistic ones of today, and it includes all sorts of accessories, from shoes to umbrellas. The star of the collection is undoubtedly 'Princess Daisy', who lies on a cushion surrounded by a wonderful array of satin and lace clothes. She was given to the future Queen Mary in 1899 for her daughter, Princess Mary.

Queen Mary was very interested in dolls' houses, and several from her collection form part of the extensive display in the central hall of the museum. Some were made as curiosities for adults, others for children, but they all give an idea of how people lived in different periods and how the houses were furnished. The earliest is the Nuremberg House from 1673, made to teach girls all about running a house. Miss Miles' Dolls' House is a massive three-storey construction from 1890, showing guests playing billiards and the servants in their cramped quarters on the top floor.

This small late-eighteenth-century dolls' house can be seen in the Bethnal Green Museum of Childhood.

BETHNAL GREEN MUSEUM OF CHILDHOOD, Cambridge Heath Road, London E2 9PA.

Telephone: 020 8983 5201.

Website: www.museumofchildhood.org.uk

Open: Saturday to Thursday 10.00–17.50. Closed Friday.

Admission free.

Nearest Underground: Bethnal Green.

Buses: 8, 26, 48, 55, 106, 253, 309, D6.

DICKENS HOUSE MUSEUM

Charles Dickens, the great nineteenth-century novelist, lived in many different houses in London, but the only one still remaining is at 48 Doughty Street, which he occupied from 1837 to 1839. The house is now a museum containing many objects relating to Dickens's life and work, such as letters, books, pictures and furniture. One of the most familiar pictures is *Dickens's Dream,* showing the writer at his desk surrounded by the ghosts of many of the best-known characters he created. You can also see the study where he wrote *Oliver Twist* and *Nicholas Nickleby* and the desk from which, towards the end of his life, he used to give public readings of his works. The drawing room where he entertained has been recreated as it was, with furniture of the period.

DICKENS HOUSE MUSEUM, 48 Doughty Street, London WC1N 2LF.

Telephone: 020 7405 2127. Fax: 020 7831 5175.

Website: www.dickensmuseum.com

Open: Monday to Saturday 10.00–17.00.

Admission charge.

Nearest Underground: Chancery Lane, Russell Square, Holborn.

Buses: 17, 19, 38, 45, 46, 55, 68, 91, 168, 188, 243.

DULWICH PICTURE GALLERY

Dulwich Picture Gallery, in suburban south London, was built in 1812 and was the very first public art gallery in Britain. It has a small, but extremely good, collection of old master paintings, including beautiful Gainsborough portraits, picturesque Murillo street urchins, Dutch landscapes and a small portrait by Rembrandt which probably holds the record for the painting most often stolen. At the heart of the gallery is its greatest curiosity, a mausoleum specially built to hold the remains of its founders. The gallery puts on a variety of special activities for children and families during the school holidays. The gallery has been totally renovated and new facilities added in a sort of cloister, including a cafe. When everyone is tired of looking at the pictures, you might enjoy some time in Dulwich Park opposite or a stroll round the streets of Dulwich, which still retains its rather elegant village atmosphere.

DULWICH PICTURE GALLERY, College Road, London SE21 7AD.

Telephone: 020 8693 5254. Fax: 020 8299 8700.

Website: www.dulwichpicturegallery.org.uk

Open: Tuesday to Friday 10.00–17.00; Saturday, Sunday and bank holidays 11.00–17.00. continued opposite

Admission charge. Children sixteen and under and students free. Friday free for everyone.

Nearest rail station: West Dulwich (from Victoria) or North Dulwich (from Cannon Street or London Bridge) plus short walk.

Buses: 3, P4, P13, P15.

FIREPOWER

Opened in May 2001 in the old Royal Arsenal, the museum tells the story of artillery and in particular of the Royal Regiment of Artillery. The displays include multimedia shows as well as real guns and missiles from the last three centuries. From Tudor times the Royal Arsenal was where arms were made and tested and its name was given to the Arsenal football team. There are lots of computers and hands-on activities as well as occasional loud explosions.

FIREPOWER, Royal Arsenal, Woolwich, London SE18 6ST.

Telephone: 020 8855 7755. Fax: 020 8855 7100.

Website: www.firepower.org.uk

Open: daily 10.00–17.00.

Admission charge.

Nearest rail station: Woolwich Arsenal (from Cannon Street and Charing Cross).

Nearest Underground: North Greenwich, then bus 161, 422 or 472 to Woolwich.

Buses: 53, 54, 161, 180, 380, 422, 472.

FLORENCE NIGHTINGALE MUSEUM

This excellent small museum tells the extraordinary story of probably the most famous nurse of all time, the so-called Lady of the Lamp. It is housed in a corner of

St Thomas's Hospital, where she founded an important school of nursing. The story of a woman who gave up her affluent lifestyle to look after those less well off than herself is told through a mixture of tableaux, models and objects, many of them once belonging to her. Among these are childhood books, her medicine chest, a nurse's uniform from the Crimea and a lantern she may have used on her visits to the wards. Although she is mostly celebrated for her work looking after the wounded and dying at the military hospital in Scutari during the Crimean War, her work back in England, setting up the nursing school and improving the way hospitals were run, was just as important. All of this is covered in the museum's displays and in the excellent

The 'Lady of the Lamp' has a whole museum dedicated to her in part of St Thomas's Hospital.

103

audio-visual presentation. There are activity sheets and questionnaires for children, and various other educational services are available.

FLORENCE NIGHTINGALE MUSEUM, 2 Lambeth Palace Road, London SE1 7EW.

Telephone: 020 7620 0374. Fax: 020 7928 1760.

Website: www.florence-nightingale.co.uk

Open: Monday to Friday 10.00–17.00; Saturday, Sunday and bank holidays 11.30–16.30.

Admission charge.

Nearest Underground: Westminster, Waterloo.

Buses: 12, 53, 77, 159, 211, 507.

GEFFRYE MUSEUM

The Geffrye Museum is housed in what were once the almshouses of the Ironmongers' Company, built in the early eighteenth century. It is the perfect setting for a series of English period rooms showing how people lived and, by means of authentic furniture, pictures, textiles and ornaments, how interior design has developed from 1600 to the present day. In December each year the rooms are decorated for Christmas in the style of each period and look particularly attractive. There are regular activities and workshops for children at weekends and during holidays.

To introduce each century there are informative display panels and a replica chair in which you are invited to sit – they get more and more comfortable with each century. The seventeenth-century rooms have sturdy oak furniture, dark wooden panelling and tapestries on the walls to keep out the draughts. By the eighteenth century the walls are painted in light colours and the furniture is more elegant, much of it made of mahogany, a wood newly imported from the West Indies. The nineteenth-century rooms, although more comfortable, are much more cluttered and highly decorated and are fitted with gas lighting, which was in general use by the 1840s.

The twentieth-century rooms are in a modern extension, which also houses a cafe, a shop and temporary exhibitions. The Edwardian room has a large wooden fireplace surround and deep, comfortable-looking armchairs, and is supplied by electricity. The 1930s flat is very plain by comparison, with little furniture or decoration. There is a 1950s space-saving open-plan room, complete with a staircase in the corner and central heating; the television has replaced the fireplace as the focus of the room. The final room, from the 1990s, is a loft conversion with the kitchen, bedroom and sitting room all created out of a single space.

Behind the museum is a series of period gardens, which are open from April to October. They are laid out in styles relating to the rooms inside and there is also a delightful herb garden.

GEFFRYE MUSEUM, Kingsland Road, London E2 8EA.

Telephone: 020 7739 9893. Fax: 020 7729 5647. Recorded information: 020 7739 8543.

Website: www.geffrye-museum.org.uk

Open: Tuesday to Saturday 10.00–17.00; Sunday and bank holidays 14.00–17.00.

Admission free.

Nearest Underground: Liverpool Street, then bus 242; or Old Street, then bus 243.

Buses: 67, 149, 242, 243.

HORNIMAN MUSEUM

The Horniman is a small and rather eccentric museum based on the collections of Frederick John Horniman, a wealthy nineteenth-century tea merchant. On his travels round the world he collected many unusual objects relating to local customs and beliefs. He had the building, with its peculiar tower, built specially to house his collection in 1901 and then gave it to the people of London as a free museum; entrance is still free today. A new extension being built during 2001 will enable more of the collection to be displayed and will house new education facilities.

There are three main sections to the museum: musical instruments; anthropology; and natural history, including an aquarium. The music collection consists of over 1500 musical instruments from around the world and from different periods, from bagpipes to panpipes, and eighteenth-century violins to 1960s electric guitars. The anthropological displays range from Egyptian mummies to bronzes from Benin in Nigeria. There is a superb collection of masks from around the world, including a Bolivian devil mask with light-bulbs for eyes, and one from Zaire made of feathers, beads and sea shells. There are also lots of puppets, including shadow puppets from Malaysia, marionettes from Burma and some nineteenth-century Punch and Judy puppets. The natural history section consists mostly of stuffed animals and birds in cases, laid out according to scientific classification. Upstairs, rather unexpectedly, is a massive nineteenth-century German 'Apostle Clock', which has scenes from the life of Christ in glass cases around the clockface. At 16.00 the apostles in the upper case move and bow to Christ, except Judas, who turns away.

A more recent addition to the museum is CUE, or Centre for Understanding the Environment, in an environmentally friendly wooden building with grass on the roof. It is aimed at younger children and has hands-on activities to teach them about the world. The gardens behind the museum have several nature trails, and there are concerts and children's shows in the summer.

HORNIMAN MUSEUM, 100 London Road, Forest Hill, London SE23 3PQ.

Telephone: 020 8699 1872. Fax: 020 8291 5506.

Website: www.horniman.demon.co.uk

Open: Monday to Saturday 10.30–17.30; Sunday 14.00–17.30.

Admission free.

Nearest rail station: Forest Hill (from London Bridge), then a five-minute walk.

Buses: 176, 185, 312, 352, P4 to the museum; 122 to Forest Hill; 63, P13 to nearby Sydenham Hill.

MUSEUM IN DOCKLANDS

Scheduled to open in late 2001, this new museum tells the fascinating story of the Thames and the development of its port from Roman times to the present day. Housed in an historic warehouse overlooking Canary Wharf, its many artefacts and interactive displays will show what life was like in the shipbuilding yards and docks of east London. Outside the museum are restored cranes, tugs and barges.

MUSEUM IN DOCKLANDS, West India Quay, London E14.

Telephone: 020 7515 1162.

Admission charge.

Nearest Underground: West India Quay (Docklands Light Railway), Canary Wharf (Jubilee Line).

Preserved cranes at the Royal Victoria Docks. The fascinating history of the London docks will be told in the new Museum in Docklands opening in 2001.

NATIONAL ARMY MUSEUM

The National Army Museum tells the story of the British army from the fifteenth century to the present day. The collections include uniforms and weapons as well as portraits and lifelike models. One of the highlights is a massive model of the Battle of Waterloo, and one of the more unusual objects is the skeleton of Napoleon's horse. Group visits can be arranged to include themed talks and the chance to handle objects from the collections. A visit to the museum can be combined with a visit to the Royal Hospital next door.

NATIONAL ARMY MUSEUM, Royal Hospital Road, London SW3 4HT.
Telephone: 020 7730 0717.
Website: www.national-army-museum.ac.uk
Open: daily 10.00–17.30.
Admission free.
Nearest Underground: Sloane Square.
Buses: 11, 19, 22, 137, 211, 239, 319.

OLD OPERATING THEATRE

This is one of London's most unusual and least known museums. It is the only surviving nineteenth-century operating theatre and was part of St Thomas's Hospital, where Florence Nightingale founded her famous nursing school. When the hospital moved to Lambeth in the nineteenth century, it was forgotten about until it was rediscovered in 1956. It has been restored and is now a fascinating little museum, providing a graphic reminder of what medical treatment was like in the days before anaesthetics.

You enter via a spiral staircase as the operating theatre was built inside the roof of a church so as to be on the same level as the ward it served. The theatre is semicircular and is surrounded by stepped areas where students stood to watch the operation. Underneath the plain wooden operating table is a box of sawdust to collect the blood, and between the floor and the roof of the church is a 3 inch (7 cm) space which was filled with sawdust to absorb the blood before it dripped into the church below. The rest of the roof space was used as a herb garret, where herbs were grown and dried for use in medicines. The displays include knives, saws and forceps used for amputations and other operations, and there are various body parts in jars.

Groups can book a guide to explain all about surgery before anaesthetics in graphic detail or, for the squeamish, talk about the work of the apothecary and the use of herbs in medicine.

> OLD OPERATING THEATRE, 9a St Thomas Street, London SE1 9RY.
> Telephone: 020 7955 4791.
> Website: www.thegarret.org.uk
> Open: daily 10.30–17.00.
> Admission charge.
> Nearest Underground: London Bridge.
> Buses: 17, 21, 35, 40, 47, 48, 133, 149, 343, 381.

POLLOCK'S TOY MUSEUM

This little museum is ideal for families as it appeals to adults and children. It is a veritable Aladdin's cave housed in two eighteenth-century houses and named after Benjamin Pollock, a Victorian toymaker famous for his toy theatres. The narrow staircases and tiny rooms are lined with glass cabinets filled with old dolls, teddy bears, dolls' houses, puppets, train sets and board games, showing how children entertained themselves in the days before television and computer games. There are also more modern displays, including Action Man and Sooty and Sweep. Many of the toys come from as far afield as India, South America, Russia and the Far East. Among the highlights are the oldest known teddy bear, called Eric, dating from 1905, a four-thousand-year-old clay mouse from Egypt, and the many and varied toy theatres with which Victorian children would bring popular stories to life. Kits based on Pollock's designs can be bought in the shop where you end your visit.

> POLLOCK'S TOY MUSEUM, 1 Scala Street, London W1P 1LT.
> Telephone: 020 7636 3452.
> Website: www.tao2000net/pollocks
> Open: Monday to Saturday (except bank holiday Mondays) 10.00–17.00.
> Admission charge.
> Nearest Underground: Goodge Street.
> Buses: 10, 24, 29, 73, 134.

ROYAL AIR FORCE MUSEUM

The Royal Air Force Museum is a must for anyone interested in the history of aviation, as it has over seventy aircraft on display at the old Hendon Aerodrome in north London. Walkways in the two huge hangars allow you to get really close to planes such as a Second World War Spitfire and a modern Harrier jet. You can even get inside a few of them, including walking through a Sunderland flying boat and sitting in the cockpit of a Jet Provost. There are lots of interactive displays as well as a flight simulator which allows you to try your hand at flying a jet. There are many special events put on throughout the year.

> ROYAL AIR FORCE MUSEUM, Grahame Park Way, London NW9 5LL.
>
> Telephone: 020 8205 2266.
>
> Website: www.rafmuseum.org.uk
>
> Open: daily 10.00–18.00.
>
> Admission charge. Senior citizens and accompanied children under sixteen free.
>
> Nearest Underground: Colindale.
>
> Bus: 303.

ROYAL HOSPITAL, CHELSEA

The Royal Hospital, Chelsea, was founded by Charles II as a home for disabled and retired soldiers. It was built by Sir Christopher Wren, who was already building St Paul's Cathedral, and opened in 1692. Over four hundred Chelsea Pensioners still live here, easily recognised by their bright red coats in summer or dark blue coats in winter. They receive free board, food and clothes as well as a weekly allowance and will often show you round the main parts of the building. In the main quadrangle is a statue of Charles II in classical armour. For the Founder's Day parade in May the statue is covered in oak branches as a reminder of Charles's narrow escape after the Battle of Worcester by hiding in an oak tree.

Through the columned porch are the chapel and the Great Hall, which are open to the public. The chapel, to the right, is still used every Sunday by the pensioners; the Great Hall, to the left, where the pensioners still have their meals, is decorated with portraits of kings and queens, including a large one at the far end of Charles II in front of the Royal Hospital. The body of the Duke of Wellington lay in state in the hall before being taken in procession for burial in St Paul's Cathedral. There is a small museum on the east side of the hospital which contains memorabilia associated with the Duke of Wellington and a display of medals awarded to hospital inmates.

> ROYAL HOSPITAL, Royal Hospital Road, London SW3 4SR.
>
> Website: www.chelseapensioner.org.uk
>
> Open: Monday to Saturday 10.00–12.00 and 14.00–16.00; Sunday 14.00–16.00.
>
> Admission free.
>
> Nearest Underground: Sloane Square.
>
> Buses: 11, 19, 22, 137, 211, 239, 319.

SIR JOHN SOANE'S MUSEUM

The architect Sir John Soane is best known for his work on the Bank of England. He built a house for himself in Lincoln's Inn Fields and filled it with his collections of antique statues, paintings and all sorts of curiosities. The museum is still much as he left it when he died, a fascinating assortment of unexpected treasures. The unusual colour schemes of some of the rooms are authentic, and the clever use of mirrors makes the rooms look larger than they really are. In the basement is the marble sarcophagus of Seti I, covered in hieroglyphic inscriptions. The most important paintings are two series by Hogarth, *The Election* and *The Rake's Progress*, which are full of fascinating and amusing details. They are housed in the unusual Picture Room where, because of the lack of space, Soane designed a room with false walls which can be opened to reveal more paintings inside. One wall even opens up to reveal a view down into the basement.

Part of the extraordinary collection of treasures in Sir John Soane's Museum.

SIR JOHN SOANE'S MUSEUM, 13 Lincoln's Inn Fields, London WC2A 3BP.

Telephone: 020 7405 2107.

Website: www.soane.org

Open: Tuesday to Saturday 10.00–17.00, plus first Tuesday in month 18.00–21.00.

Admission free.

Nearest Underground: Holborn.

Buses: 8, 25, 59, 68, 91, 168, 171, 188, 242, 243, 501, 521.

WALLACE COLLECTION

The Wallace Collection, one of London's less visited attractions, is a wonderful collection of paintings, porcelain and furniture, much of it from eighteenth-century France, including items once belonging to Queen Marie Antoinette. There is also a fine collection of European and oriental armour. The most famous picture is Frans Hals' *Laughing Cavalier.* The gallery puts on lots of special events for children and families, such as concerts, story-telling and the chance to try on armour. These need to be booked in advance.

WALLACE COLLECTION, Hertford House, Manchester Square, London W1M 6BN.

Telephone: 020 7563 9500. Education department: 020 7563 9551.

Website: www.wallace-collection.com

Open: Monday to Saturday 10.00–17.00; Sunday 14.00–17.00.

Admission free.

Nearest Underground: Bond Street.

Buses: 2, 6, 7, 10, 12, 13, 15, 23, 30, 73, 74, 82, 94, 98, 113, 137, 139, 159, 189, 274.

The spacious quadrangle of the Royal Hospital, Chelsea.

A Chelsea Pensioner collecting for the Army Benevolent Fund.

WIMBLEDON LAWN TENNIS MUSEUM

Although it is not the easiest place to get to, those with a keen interest in tennis will enjoy a visit to this museum, which is right at the heart of the club where the world's most famous tournament is played every year on its grass courts. The displays show how the sport evolved from the medieval game of real (or royal) tennis, with collections of memorabilia, costumes, archive film and interactive quizzes. You can also see the celebrated Centre Court and the original trophies presented to the winners each year.

WIMBLEDON LAWN TENNIS MUSEUM, All England Lawn Tennis and Croquet Club, Church Road, London SW19 5AE.

Telephone: 020 8946 6131. Fax: 020 8944 6497.

Website: www.wimbledon.org

Open: daily 10.30–17.00.

Admission charge.

Closed Friday to Sunday before the Championships, and open only to those with tickets during the tournament.

Nearest Underground: Southfields, then fifteen-minute walk.

Buses: 39, 93, 200.

29
Greenwich

Greenwich, a small town on the river Thames 5 miles (8 km) downstream of Tower Bridge, has important connections with British maritime history. It has several attractions which between them tell the story of Britain's relationship with the sea. To take advantage of all that Greenwich has to offer, you need to allow a full day for your visit.

The quickest way to Greenwich is by train from Charing Cross, which takes about twenty minutes. However, if you can spare the time, it is worth taking either a river boat or the Docklands Light Railway, as there is much to see on the way there. A boat trip from central London takes about forty-five minutes and is accompanied by a commentary telling you about everything you see on the way. There are good views of all the new developments along the river, among them the massive Canary Wharf Tower, the tallest building in Britain. Arriving this way also allows you to enjoy the view of Greenwich from the river, one of the best views in London. To see more of the redeveloped Docklands area you could take the Docklands Light Railway from either Bank or Tower Gateway. The trains run on overhead tracks, so you get to see even more of the area and its interesting mixture of old and new buildings. The route takes you into Canary Wharf and on to the bottom end of the Isle of Dogs, where the trains drop into a tunnel under the Thames, bringing you out at Cutty Sark station, from where you can start your visit to Greenwich. You could get out at Island Gardens station before going under the Thames to enjoy the view of Greenwich across the river, and either take the next train or walk under the Thames through the old foot tunnel.

The sight of the **Cutty Sark** in a dry dock by the Thames sets the nautical tone straight away. The ship is the last surviving tea clipper from the nineteenth century,

and is a very elegant vessel, with 11 miles (17.7 km) of rigging, which once held 32,000 square feet (2973 square metres) of sail. She was one of the ships that took part in the annual race to bring the first of the tea crop from China to England, and she later carried wool from Australia until the faster steamships took over. In 1954 the *Cutty Sark* was saved for the nation and now houses an exhibition about life on board and a collection of ships' figureheads. The ship's own figurehead explains its rather unusual name, which comes from the poem 'Tam O'Shanter' by Robert Burns – its shows a rather attractive witch wearing a short shirt (the 'cutty sark') and holding the tail of Tam's horse.

The famous tea clipper Cutty Sark in dry dock at Greenwich.

CUTTY SARK, King William Walk, London SE10 9HT.
Telephone: 020 8858 3445. Fax: 020 8853 3589.
Website: www.cuttysark.org.uk
Open: daily 10.00–17.00.
Admission charge.

Next to the *Cutty Sark*, but not open to the public, is the tiny boat **Gipsy Moth IV**, in which Sir Francis Chichester sailed round the world in 1966–7. It is extraordinary to think that he could have spent 226 days at sea in such a tiny vessel. He was knighted by the Queen here at Greenwich with the same sword Elizabeth I used to knight Sir Francis Drake, who sailed round the globe in the *Golden Hinde*, a replica of which is berthed on the Thames beside Southwark Cathedral (see Chapter 25).

A short walk brings you to the entrance of what was the **Royal Naval College**. It is a very grand building and was originally built by Sir Christopher Wren as a naval hospital along the lines of the Royal Hospital in Chelsea. On the site there was once a royal palace called Placentia, where both Henry VIII and Elizabeth I were born. The naval college has now moved away and been replaced by Greenwich University, but the chapel and Great Hall are open to the public. The Great Hall is better known as the Painted Hall, as its walls and ceiling are covered in paintings by Sir James Thornhill, who painted the inside of the dome of St Paul's Cathedral. On the ceiling are William III and Mary II, who commissioned the building, and on the far wall are George I and his family. It was in this hall that the body of Nelson lay in state after it was brought back from Trafalgar in 1805, before being carried up the Thames to be buried in St Paul's.

OLD ROYAL NAVAL COLLEGE, Romney Road, London SE10 9LS.
Telephone: 020 8269 4747. Fax: 020 8269 4757.
Website: www.greenwichfoundation.org.uk
Open: Monday to Saturday 10.00–17.00; Sunday and bank holidays 12.30–17.00. May close occasionally at short notice.
Admission charge (under sixteen free). Free after 15.30 and all day Sunday.

The **National Maritime Museum** is the largest museum of its kind in the world and deals with Britain's nautical connections, covering such subjects as piracy, slavery, exploration, naval battles and ecology. Among the many objects you can see are scale models of famous ships, historic vessels, navigational instruments, and many important Nelson relics.

The main entrance is on Romney Road and it leads you straight into the spacious Neptune Court. Around the sides of the court are three 'streets', which contain several interesting boats. In East Street, to the left, is *Suhaili*, the yacht in which Robin Knox-Johnston won the Golden Globe round-the-world race in 1968–9. In doing so, he became the first person to sail single-handed non-stop around the globe. Close by is *Miss Britain III*, which was the first powerboat to reach 100 mph (185 km/h), winning the world sea mile record in 1934. In South Street is the splendidly ornate royal barge made for Prince Frederick, the eldest son of George II. It is painted in red and gold and is covered in dolphins and seashells, with a crown on top of the cabin. It must have created quite an impression as it sailed up and down the Thames. Frederick was never to inherit the throne of England, as he died young after being hit by a cricket ball. On the wall above the barge is the stern and figurehead of the *Implacable*, a French ship captured at the Battle of Trafalgar. For many years she was used as a boys' training ship, but in 1949 she had to be scuttled in the English Channel as it was too expensive to repair her.

Around the 'streets' are a number of special displays. The main ones on this level relate to the explorers, from the Vikings' discovery of North America to the

George I and his family on the wall of the Painted Hall in the Royal Naval College at Greenwich.

exploration of the polar regions. There are many fascinating relics of these voyages, including a post placed at the magnetic North Pole in 1831 and relics from Franklin's attempt to find the North-West Passage, an expedition from which no-one returned. A banjo played by Hussey during the 800 mile (1287 km) journey in a lifeboat, and signed by members of the crew, is a relic of Shackleton's ill-fated 1915 expedition when the *Endurance* was trapped by ice. Also on display are a sextant used by Captain Cook and a coconut cup given by Sir Francis Drake to Elizabeth I after he had sailed round the world in 1577–80 – coconuts had never been seen in England before. There are also a number of poignant items found in Captain Scott's tent after the doomed journey to the South Pole in 1910–12 in which all the team members died. They include a reindeer-hide sleeping bag, ration bags and the stove on which they made their last hot drink.

The Passengers display tells the story of the great ocean liners and of the people who travelled in them, many to start a new life in a new land. One of the greatest was the *Mauretania* of 1907; first- and third-class cabins have been recreated to give an idea of what life on board was like. There are also some impressive models of five passenger ships, including the 109,000 ton *Grand Princess*, which, when it was launched in 1998, was the largest and most expensive cruise ship ever built.

The Rank and File gallery has been cleverly designed to display uniforms through the ages, complete with a video showing how nautical styles have influenced the modern fashion industry. Along both sides of the room are wardrobes which you open to see the various uniforms, ranging from that of an eighteenth-century lieutenant to a modern sub-aqua suit. Among them is the sailor suit of Prince Albert Edward, the future Edward VII, which became a very fashionable outfit for boys and girls as well as adults.

The Trade and Empire exhibition shows how the British Empire was created for seaborne trading, including that of human cargoes in the slave trade. The displays show how the demand for sugar, tea and cotton in the drawing rooms of Britain relied on the use of African slaves working in the plantations of the West Indies. The Seapower display uses paintings, models and videos to portray naval and merchant shipping in the twentieth century, and the Art and the Sea gallery has a fine collection of maritime paintings, from seventeenth-century Dutch pictures to contemporary British art.

One of the highlights of the museum is the Nelson gallery, which tells the story of Britain's greatest naval hero, with many personal items and trophies taken from enemy ships. He entered the navy aged only twelve and, despite suffering from seasickness throughout his life, rose quickly through the ranks. Several battles are described, with an audio-visual display on the Battle of Trafalgar, in which he died, shot by a French sniper. The coat and blood-stained breeches he was wearing when he was shot are also on display (you can see the bullet hole in the shoulder of the coat). There is a recreation of the home he shared in Merton with his mistress, Emma Hamilton, and a display of many of the commemorative souvenirs made since his death. A special Cabinet of Curiosities has drawers containing unusual facts about Nelson: for example, despite the stories to the contrary, he never wore an eyepatch but had a shade to protect his good eye. There is also a special combination knife and fork he had made when he lost his right arm.

NATIONAL MARITIME MUSEUM, Greenwich, London SE10 9NF.

Telephone: 020 8312 6565. Fax: 020 8312 6632.

Website: www.nmm.ac.uk

Open: daily 10.00–17.00.

Admission charge (children under sixteen and senior citizens free). Free for all from December 2001.

A combined ticket is available which includes admission to the Royal Observatory.

Behind the museum is Greenwich Park, the oldest of London's Royal Parks. Up on the hill is the **Royal Observatory**, which was built for Charles II by Wren to house the first Astronomer Royal. This is where you will find the line of the Prime Meridian, from where time is measured. There is a museum here on the measurement of time and on the work of John Harrison, who found a way of calculating longitude at sea that was to save many lives. You can also visit the Octagon Room, with its tall windows that allowed the use of long telescopes to study the heavens. There are extensive views from here down over Greenwich, across to Docklands and the Canary Wharf Tower and down river to the spectacular Dome. The Dome, with its massive curved roof, the largest in the world, was created to celebrate the millennium in 2000.

ROYAL OBSERVATORY, Greenwich, London SE10 9NF.

Telephone: 020 8312 6565.

Website: www.rog.nmm.ac.uk

Open: daily 10.00–17.00.

Admission charge (children under sixteen and senior citizens free). Free for all from December 2001.

A combined ticket includes entrance to the National Maritime Museum.

River boats from Greenwich take you further downstream to the **Thames Barrier**, which opened in 1984 to prevent London from being flooded (the last flood was in 1953). The barrier consists of ten massive gates which normally sit on the river bed, allowing boats to pass through, but they can be raised in an emergency to stop the flow of water. The electro-hydraulic machinery used to move the gates is housed in the giant steel-covered piers. On the south bank is a visitor centre which describes the barrier's construction and operation, with audio-visual displays and a working model.

THAMES BARRIER VISITOR CENTRE, 1 Unity Way, London SE18 5NJ.

Telephone: 020 8305 4188. Fax: 020 8855 2146.

Open: daily 10.30–16.30.

Admission charge.

Nearest rail station: Charlton (from Cannon Street, Charing Cross or London Bridge), then a fifteen-minute walk.

Buses: 177, 180.

By river from Westminster and Greenwich.

30
Kew

Kew is an attractive suburb of south-west London best-known for its famous botanical garden, but there are also two small museums which may be of interest to families with older children.

Kew Gardens or, more correctly, the Royal Botanic Gardens, Kew, cover an area of over 300 acres (more than 120 hectares) and house the most extensive collection of plants anywhere in the world. Partly because of the glasshouses, there is something of interest to see at any time of year. The first botanical garden here was created in 1759 by George III's mother, Princess Augusta, who lived in Kew Palace, which still stands in a corner of the gardens. She had a number of buildings added, including several 'ruins' and the Chinese pagoda. The gardens were given to the nation in 1841 and extended to their present size, and the collection now consists of about 40,000 different plants. The gardens are also an important centre for scientific research.

There are several entrances to the gardens, but from Kew Gardens Underground station you will arrive at the Victoria Gate, where you will find a visitor centre, a coffee shop and the main shop. A short walk from here brings you to the famous Palm House, a vast greenhouse overlooking an ornamental lake. The atmosphere inside is hot and very humid as it contains plants from the tropical rainforest, including palms and rubber trees. There is a colourful display of coral and fish in the basement. On the opposite side of the lake is an exhibition called 'Plants + People', which looks at the way plants affect our lives.

Several other glasshouses house different kinds of plants, including the Alpine House, the Waterlily House and the enormous Temperate House, which contains citrus trees and a Chilean wine palm, the world's largest indoor plant. The ultra-modern Princess of Wales Conservatory is named after both Augusta, Princess of Wales, who founded the gardens, and Diana, Princess of Wales, who opened the building in 1987. It was specially built to display plants from ten different climates, from the cacti of the arid deserts to the colourful and exotic orchids from the tropics. Also here is the spectacular giant Amazon waterlily, whose leaves grow to nearly 9 feet (3 metres) across.

There is something to see in Kew Gardens at any time of the year. The magnolias and azaleas appear in springtime, the Rhododendron Dell is ablaze with colour in June and the autumn colours are usually spectacular. One of the biggest attractions are the bluebell woods around Queen Charlotte's Cottage in May.

ROYAL BOTANIC GARDENS, Kew, Richmond, Surrey TW9 3AB.
Telephone: 020 8940 1171.
Website: www.rbgkew.org.uk
Open: daily from 9.30. Last entry times 15.30–19.30 depending on time of year.
Admission charge.
Nearest Underground: Kew Gardens.
Buses: 65, 391, 419.

On the other side of the river is the **Kew Bridge Steam Museum**. Cross Kew Bridge and turn left into Kew Bridge Road, where you will see a tall tower. This is

The Palm House in Kew Gardens contains plants from the tropics.

the old Grand Junction Water Works pumping station, which now houses the museum, where you can see an amazing collection of steam and diesel engines of all shapes and sizes. Anyone with an interest in machines and how they work will enjoy a visit, especially at weekends and bank holidays, when many of them can be seen operating, and volunteer guides explain their workings. The five original Cornish beam engines are still there, and the gigantic 90 inch (2286 mm) engine is the biggest working beam engine in the world. You can walk up to a viewing platform to stand next to the massive 32 ton beam and when the engine is in steam its power is awesome. In their heyday these engines could pump 30 million gallons (more than 136 million litres) of water into the reservoirs every day.

The Water for Life exhibition puts all this in context by telling the story of London's water supply and sewerage system from Roman times to the present day. There are lots of hands-on activities, with buttons to push and levers to pull. You can find out about the 'flushers', whose job was to clean out the sewers, and the 'toshers', who made a living by going down into them to scavenge whatever they could find.

KEW BRIDGE STEAM MUSEUM, Green Dragon Lane, Brentford, Middlesex TW8 0EN.

Telephone: 020 8568 4757.

Website: www.kbsm.org.uk

Open: daily 11.00–17.00 (engines operate weekends and bank holiday Mondays).

Admission charge.

Nearest Underground: Gunnersbury, then 237 or 267 bus; Kew Gardens, then 391 bus.

Nearest rail station: Kew Bridge (from Waterloo).

Buses: 65, 237, 267, 391.

Only a short distance along the same road is one of London's most unusual and delightful museums, the **Musical Museum**. Housed in a disused church, which lends it a special charm, it consists of an extraordinary collection of automatic musical instruments. This is not just a dry, stuffy museum with objects in glass cases, because most of them still work, and the guides demonstrate a wide variety of different instruments which were developed long before the days of the CD and Walkman. If you are lucky, you may even get the chance to try some of them yourselves.

The music ranges from popular songs on a barrel piano that would be wheeled

The Chinese pagoda in Kew Gardens.

around the streets, to piano rolls of famous jazz and classical pianists that could be played in the privacy of your own home. The museum has a wonderful collection of player pianos, which use paper rolls to play what is actually a very accurate 'recording' of performances by celebrated pianists of the past. One of these pianos once belonged to Queen Victoria's youngest daughter, Beatrice. There are also instruments called orchestrions, which sound like an orchestra with various percussion instruments and added lighting effects, and a clever machine which plays a real violin accompanied by a piano. The most spectacular instrument in the collection is a 'Mighty Wurlitzer' organ from the 1930s, which used to be a star attraction in a cinema in Kingston upon Thames. It would rise impressively out of the floor during the intermission to entertain cinema-goers, with bright glass panels changing colour throughout the performance. It no longer moves, but its hundreds of organ pipes, percussion instruments including drums and bells, and a number of special effects, all create a most impressive sound during the demonstration.

MUSICAL MUSEUM, 368 High Street, Brentford, Middlesex TW8 0BD.

Telephone: 020 8560 8108.

Open: April to October, Saturday to Sunday 14.00–17.00, also Wednesday 14.00–16.00 during July and August.

Admission charge.

Nearest Underground: Gunnersbury, then 237 or 267 bus.

Nearest rail station: Kew Bridge (from Waterloo).

Buses: 65, 237, 267.

31
Hampton Court Palace

As royal palaces go, Hampton Court has just about everything. There is so much to see and do that you could easily spend a whole day here. As well as the sumptuous royal apartments, there are the Tudor kitchens to explore, acres of gardens to wander around and, of course, the famous maze in which to get lost. Costumed guides take you round some of the rooms, explaining what they were used for and bringing alive for the visitor what life at court was like. If you prefer it, there are also taped commentaries for hire. Special events are often arranged, especially at holiday times, so check all this out at the information point.

The oldest part of the palace dates from the Tudor period. It was given to Henry VIII by his Chancellor, Cardinal Wolsey, who had fallen out of favour, and the king turned it into an opulent palace big enough for himself and his many courtiers. In the late seventeenth century William III and Mary II decided they wanted something more modern and they commissioned Sir Christopher Wren to design a new palace in the latest style. As the money ran out, some of the Tudor palace was left as it was, so that today's building is rather like two different palaces. In 1986 a bad fire damaged parts of the palace, but the rooms have been restored to their former splendour.

The main entrance is through the Tudor gatehouse, which leads into the large Base Court and then through into the smaller Clock Court. Look out for the **Astronomical Clock**, made for Henry VIII, showing the sun going round the Earth, which was what scientists believed at the time. It also shows the time of high tide at London Bridge, which was very important as Henry travelled to and from the palace by river. Henry's apartments include the magnificent **Great Hall**, which has a wonderful wooden roof. Look carefully and you will see lots of carved and painted heads on the beams. This room was where the courtiers would have eaten. You can also visit the Chapel Royal and the Royal Pew, where Henry would follow the service going on down below. The corridor outside the chapel is known as the Haunted Gallery. Before being taken to the Tower to be executed, Henry's fifth wife, Catherine Howard, was kept at Hampton Court. She tried to get into the chapel to plead with Henry for her life, but she was caught by the guards and dragged down the gallery screaming. Her ghost has been seen here on several occasions.

The vast **Tudor Kitchens** were built to cater for the more than one thousand people who attended Henry VIII. On the way in there is a model explaining the layout of the different areas. The various rooms are laid out with authentic-looking furniture, utensils and ingredients, as if a banquet were being prepared. At the heart are the three Great Kitchens, where you can see a huge open fire with a spit for roasting the meat – it would have been turned by young boys, who must have had a very hot and unpleasant job. In those days three-quarters of the diet was meat and Henry's court could get through over eight thousand sheep and nearly two thousand pigs in a year.

The entrance to the **King's Apartments**, created for William III, is up a very grand staircase with colourful paintings all over the walls and ceiling. It was painted by an Italian artist, Antonio Verrio, and shows all sorts of classical gods and heroes, flattering the king by likening him to the great warrior Alexander the Great. The apartments are a sequence of rooms, starting with the more ornate public ones, where the king would hold audiences, and ending with the private chambers, which only the king's most intimate friends and courtiers could enter. Look out for the

The Tudor kitchen at Hampton Court.

King's stoolroom, or toilet, which contains Charles II's 'close stool', with its velvet seat.

The **Queen's Apartments** were made for Mary II, but she died before they were finished and much of the decoration was made for Queen Anne. The most impressive room is the Queen's Drawing Room, decorated with paintings by Verrio, showing Queen Anne on one wall receiving homage from all four corners of the globe and on the ceiling enthroned as Justice. Her husband, Prince George of Denmark, appears on one wall in armour as Admiral of the Fleet and on the opposite wall, rather awkwardly, riding naked on the back of a dolphin.

The **Georgian Rooms** are the private apartments made for George II and Queen Caroline and their large family. They are less grand and formal than the earlier rooms. The Queen's Private Bedchamber was the most private room in the palace. It had special locks in the doors which allowed the king and queen to lock themselves in away from servants and courtiers. In the morning they could pull a cord by the bedside to unlock the doors.

After your tour inside there are 60 acres (24 hectares) or so of gardens surrounding the palace in which to relax. From Wren's elegant Fountain Court you emerge into the East Gardens, with their colourful flowerbeds and yew trees over three hundred years old. Beyond is a canal known as Long Water. Turn right and right again into the formal **Privy Garden**, created for William III as his private garden and visible from his apartments. Beyond are three smaller gardens which are a riot of colour in spring and summer. At the end is the Great Vine, which, planted in 1768, is the oldest known vine in the world and still produces a good crop of grapes every year, some of which are sold in the shop. Return to the East Front and head for the Northern Gardens. On the way you will pass the Royal Tennis Court, where real (or royal) tennis has been played since the 1620s. Unlike lawn tennis, it is played indoors with a heavy leather ball, which is often hit off the walls, rather like squash.

The Fountain Court at Hampton Court.

If you are lucky you may be able to watch the game being played. The Northern Gardens are wilder than the others, and in spring the grass is covered with an impressive carpet of flowers. This is also where you will find the famous **maze**, which was created in 1702 for King William, and is still one of Hampton Court's most popular attractions.

HAMPTON COURT PALACE, East Molesey, Surrey KT8 9AU.

Telephone: 020 8781 9500. Fax: 020 8781 9669.

Website: www.hrp.org.uk

Open: April to October, 09.30–18.00 (Mondays 10.15–18.00); November to March, 09.30–16.30 (Mondays 10.15–16.30).

Admission charge.

Nearest Underground: Richmond, then R68 bus.

Nearest rail station: Hampton Court (from Waterloo).

Buses: 111, 216, 411, 416, 451, 461, 513, 726, R68.

32
Windsor

Although not actually in London, a visit to Windsor is a popular day trip from London, the famous castle itself offering plenty of interest. There are several ways of getting to Windsor from London. The quickest is by train from Paddington, changing at Slough. This brings you into Windsor Central station, right opposite the castle. The slower, stopping, train from Waterloo arrives at Windsor Riverside station at the bottom of the hill. Another option is to take a Green Line bus, which drops you off in the High Street. A number of sightseeing tour companies offer guided tours of Windsor, sometimes combined with Hampton Court (Chapter 31) or Runnymede (see page 6 for details of tour companies).

Whichever way you travel, you will be able to see the impressive bulk of **Windsor Castle** long before you get there. The first, wooden, castle was built by William I in about 1080 as part of a ring of castles to defend the capital of the country he had just conquered. Its location on a hill overlooking the Thames made it relatively easy to defend. A stone castle soon replaced the wooden one, and later the castle became a royal residence, where the monarch could entertain the Court and important visitors. Nearly every monarch has added something to the castle, but the way it looks today is due to the massive restorations carried out for George IV. The castle is still a favourite of the Queen, who regularly spends weekends there. When she is in residence the Royal Standard flies on top of the Round Tower; at other times the Union Flag flies. On 20th November 1992 a serious fire destroyed or damaged many of the state rooms, but these have now been restored to their former glory.

Once inside the castle you pass, on the right, the Round Tower, where William's original castle stood. The stone tower was built by Henry II, but the top half was added by George IV to make it look more impressive. Go through an arch on to the

Guardsmen on parade at Windsor Castle.

North Terrace, where there are excellent views across to Eton and its famous school, Eton College. On the right is the entrance to the State Apartments and Queen Mary's Dolls' House.

Queen Mary's Dolls' House is one of the most spectacular examples ever made. It was created as a present for Queen Mary in 1924 and was the work of the most important designers, artists and craftsmen of the period. It depicts a royal palace in all its aspects, from the sumptuous main rooms to the servants' quarters, as well as a garden and an underground garage with vintage cars. Everything was recreated in the most amazing detail, from the carpets and furniture to the sewing machine and wine bottles, and even the books were specially written by famous authors such as Rudyard Kipling and Arthur Conan Doyle. Many of the objects, such as the lift, really work, and hot and cold water can run from the taps.

Entry to the **State Apartments** is up the Grand Staircase. At the top of the stairs are two suits of boy's armour, made for James I's eldest son, Henry, Prince of Wales. In one of the cases you will find a curious doorlock which fired two bullets at anyone who tried to tamper with it. The next room is the Waterloo Chamber, created to remember the defeat of Napoleon at Waterloo in 1815. Around the walls are portraits of important people who helped in his defeat, including, high up on the far wall, the Duke of Wellington.

The next few rooms were created for Charles II and are now hung with some of the finest paintings from the royal collection. In the King's Dressing Room is Van Dyck's famous triple portrait of Charles I, painted from three angles, to be sent to Rome for the great sculptor Bernini to make his bust. One of the finest of the rooms is the King's Dining Room, where food appears in all the decoration. On the ceiling is a painting of a banquet of the gods, and on the frieze underneath are lifelike paintings of fruit, game birds, fish and a wonderful lobster. The carved flowers, fruit and vegetables were made by Grinling Gibbons, the most famous woodcarver of the period. Look out for the peapods, which according to tradition he carved open only if he had been paid.

The Queen's Ballroom is hung with more portraits by Van Dyck, including one of five of Charles I's children with a huge dog. The Queen's Guard Chamber has decorative displays of swords and pistols on the walls. The carved ivory throne was a gift to Queen Victoria from the Maharajah of Travancore. The French flags on display are presented to the Queen each year by the Dukes of Marlborough and Wellington in payment of rent for their estates, which were given to their ancestors in recognition of their great military victories at Blenheim and Waterloo.

The next few rooms are those restored or rebuilt after the fire of 1992. First is St George's Hall, which was one of the most badly damaged. It has a new oak hammerbeam roof, decorated with the coats of arms of every Knight of the Garter since the order was founded in 1348. The blank shields represent a knight who fell out of favour and had the honour taken away. The names of the knights are on panels round the walls. At the far end is an armoured figure on horseback. This is the King's Champion, who used to ride into the coronation banquet and challenge anyone to deny the new king. The Lantern Lobby beyond used to be the Private Chapel, and it was here the fire started. The huge suit of armour was made for Henry VIII, who was 6 feet (183 cm) tall.

Next comes the glittering Grand Reception Room, where the Queen meets her guests before a banquet. It was created for George IV and is full of dazzling gilt plasterwork. The Garter Throne Room is where new Knights of the Garter are invested with the order, whose insignia can be seen in the ceiling. The last room is the Waterloo Chamber; you passed through here before, but you can now take a proper look at the portraits, which include royalty, politicians, military leaders and the Pope.

After you leave the State Apartments walk back down past the Round Tower and on into the Lower Ward, where you will find **St George's Chapel.** The chapel was started by Edward IV. It is built in Perpendicular Gothic style and has a beautiful fan-vaulted ceiling. As a royal burial place the chapel is second only to Westminster Abbey. There are marble tombs to Edward VII and George V with their queens and in the vaults under the choir are buried Henry VIII with his third wife, Jane Seymour, Charles I, George III, George IV and William IV. The chapel is home to the Order of the Garter, the oldest order of chivalry in Britain. By tradition it was created in 1348 when, at a ball, the Countess of Salisbury, Edward III's mistress, dropped her garter. The king picked it up and put it on his own leg, saying '*Honi soit qui mal y pense*' ('Shame on him who thinks ill of it'), and this is the motto of the order. He added that the garter would soon be something they would all be honoured to wear. There are twenty-four Knights and their standards hang above their stalls in the choir, along with a helmet and sword. On the backs of the stalls are nearly seven hundred plaques of Garter Knights. Every year in June there is a Garter Day service, attended by the Queen, when new Knights are installed. Outside the east end of the chapel is the Albert Memorial Chapel, designed for Queen Victoria to commemorate her beloved husband, Prince Albert, who died at Windsor of typhoid in 1861, aged only forty-two.

At the bottom of the slope is an open area where the Changing the Guard ceremony takes place at 11.00 most days, but not on Sundays.

WINDSOR CASTLE, Windsor, Berkshire SL4 1NJ.

Telephone: 01753 831118.

Website: www.royalresidences.com

Open: March to October, 9.45–17.15; November–February 9.45–16.15.

Admission charge.

Nearest rail stations: Windsor Central (from Paddington); Windsor Riverside (from Waterloo).

Buses: Green Line 702.

St George's Chapel closed Sundays.

A short walk will bring you to the river Thames, where a footbridge takes you across to the small town of Eton, famous for its public school, **Eton College**, where Prince William and Prince Harry have been educated. The High Street is very attractive, with some interesting old houses. The school is at the end on the right. It can be visited at certain times, and there are a couple of options: an unguided visit allows access to the main quadrangle, cloister, chapel and Museum of Eton Life, which tells the history of the school and illustrates daily life there; a guided tour covers more and allows you to see inside part of the old school.

ETON COLLEGE, Windsor, Berkshire SL4 6DW.

Telephone: 01753 671177. Fax: 01753 671265.

Website: www.etoncollege.com

Open: mid March to mid April and July to August 10.30–16.30; from mid April to June and also September 14.00–16.30.

Admission charge. Extra charge for guided tours at 14.15 and 15.15.

A more modern attraction near Windsor is **Legoland**, which is aimed at children aged two to twelve. As well as the famous recreation of European cities in Lego

Lego Racer is an exciting attraction at Legoland.

bricks, there are lots of special rides and hands-on activities, such as a chance to learn to drive or pan for gold. It is both fun and educational, and you should allow a full day to take advantage of all that is on offer.

LEGOLAND, Windsor, Berkshire SL4 4AY.

Telephone: 08705 040404.

Website: www.legoland.co.uk

Open: daily from mid March to October 10.00–18.00.

Admission charge.

By road Legoland is on the B3022 Windsor–Ascot road, 2 miles (3.2 km) from Windsor.

By bus: there is a bus service from both railway stations at Windsor. Golden Tours offer a coach service from London (telephone: 020 7233 7030).

Big Ben in Miniland London is part of Legoland's recreation of European cities.

Further reading

Baker, Margaret. *London Statues and Monuments.* Shire, fifth edition 2002.

Maynard, Christopher, and Bailey, Jacqui. *The Story of London.* A. & C. Black, 2000.

Mills, A.D. *Dictionary of London Place Names.* Oxford University Press, 2001.

Sumeray, Derek. *Discovering London Plaques.* Shire, 1999.

Tames, Richard. *A Traveller's History of London.* Windrush Press, 1992.

Wittich, John. *Discovering Off-Beat Walks in London.* Shire, 2001.

Wittich, John. *Discovering London Curiosities.* Shire, 1997.

The British Library has a large piazza dominated by a statue of Sir Isaac Newton.

Index